THE TIMES IN RHYMES

The 100 moments of British History that everyone should know

The Times in Rhymes *is available in paperback and on Kindle at Amazon*

Horizons New Publishing Ltd
42-44 Copthorne Road
Felbridge, RH19 2NS
United Kingdom

Website: www.horizonsnew.com

Cover Illustrations by Susan Harrison
SOOZIHUMOR
www.susanharrison.biz

The future begins with the past

CONTENTS

FOREWORD

A recent survey of young British adults found that less than half were able to identify Winston Churchill as Britain's World War II leader. Surveys such this inspired me to create this book, because as Edmund Burke famously put it: "*Those who do not know history are doomed to repeat it*". Without doubt, some knowledge of the past is needed by everyone in a democratic country - which depends upon people being able to make sensible choices on who is going to govern us come election time.

The Times in Rhymes provides the 100 moments of the last 1,000 years of British history that everyone should know, in short memorable headlines. It also describes the background to each in just 300 words of plain English. In this fashion, I have made getting to know the essentials of our history as easy as possible. I really hope that you enjoy it.

Before you start, a quick word about dates. As most of you will know, the numbers we give our years are based on the number of years after Jesus Christ was said to have been born. So, the year 2020, was the $2,020^{th}$ year after that date. We call it AD 2020, where AD stands for the Latin term *Anno Domini,* which means in English "*in the year of the Lord*". "*The Lord*" is a name Christians give to Jesus Christ. The years before Jesus Christ are called BC, or Before Christ. For example, if we refer to 1000 BC, we are talking about more than 3,000 years ago. People are also often confused by the use of the term Century. The first hundred years after Jesus Christ was born is called the First Century – in other words the period from AD 1 to AD 100, the Second Century is from 101 to 200, and so on. The Eleventh Century is therefore 1001-1100, and the Twentieth Century is 1901 to 2000.

Peter Hodkin.

In the beginning...

After Stone Age man emerged from caves

Britain was ruled by a series of waves

In the beginning...

The one interesting fact about history, that everyone agrees, is that it is really short. History is said to have begun less than 5,500 years ago - when writing was first invented in Mesopotamia, around the area of modern-day Iraq. The time before that is called pre-history. Accordingly, when pre-historic man is referred to, this could mean just fifty-five 100-year life spans ago.

Modern humans, known as *homo sapiens,* are believed to have first appeared on Earth about 315,000 years ago. Prior to that different human species existed, the last of which probably died out about 40,000 years ago. The period we call the Stone Age, named after the fact that human species used tools made from stone, started about 2.6 million years ago and ended about 5,500 years ago – in other words at the start of what we now call history. The Stone Age was followed by the Bronze Age. Bronze was made by melting, mixing and shaping lumps of copper and tin ore in a hot fire, and widely used to make tools and weapons. The Bronze Age was followed by the Iron Age, from about 3,200 years ago – when tools and weapons were made from iron or steel. Steel was made by combining iron with other elements, and was stronger than Bronze. The Bronze and Iron Ages started at different times in different places around the world. In Britain the Bronze Age started about 4,500 years ago. It ended, and the Iron Age began, about 2,800 years ago.

While humans have always lived in communities and tribes, the invention of superior weapons and technologies enabled these communities to grow in size, and to dominate and enslave neighbouring communities. Great migrations occurred, as tribes sought to conquer others or avoid being conquered, and generally to find better places to farm and live.

Until about 8,500 years ago Britain was physically joined to the rest of Europe on its south eastern side, which had allowed a very free movement of people. But, at that time, rising sea levels submerged a large area of land, joining the North Sea to the English Channel, and Britain became the island we know today.

The existence of the ring of huge carved stones that make up the ancient monument known as Stonehenge, in Wiltshire, indicates that those who were responsible for its construction, from about 5,000 years ago, were well organised. Its 100 or so stones, each weighing over 25 tons, had been transported about 200 miles to this site.

People we now call Ancient Britons, or Celtic Britons, migrated from mainland Europe about 2,800 years ago, bringing the Iron Age with them. They conquered and subsumed the earlier peoples. They were, in turn, conquered by the Romans just under 2,000 years ago, in what we now call AD 43. After seeing off a revolt of Celtic tribes led by the legendary Queen Boadicea, in AD 60, England was ruled by Rome for nearly 400 years. The Roman Empire occupied much of Europe, Northern Africa and the Middle East, and introduced a level of civilisation to Britain never before seen, which is still evident in many parts today in ancient ruins and roads. The period after the Romans left is known as the Dark Ages, as civilisation, and the level of technology in use, dramatically deteriorated.

The next major invasion of England was by Saxon, Angle and Jute tribes from Northern Germany and Denmark, from about 1,550 years ago, or the 5th Century. Collectively they became known as Anglo-Saxons, or English Saxons, and the language they spoke is known as Old English. They dominated the Ancient Britons and other peoples living in England. The Angles created kingdoms known as East Anglia and West Anglia, the latter becoming known as Mercia. East, west and south Saxon kingdoms, were called Essex, Wessex and Sussex. The Jutes created the kingdom of Kent. Northumbria later became an Anglo-Saxon kingdom of people living north of the River Humber. A united kingdom of England was eventually created in AD 927 under King Æthelstan , largely due to the earlier efforts of the Wessex King, Alfred the Great, who lived from AD 848 to 899.

11ᵗʰ CENTURY

In the 11ᵗʰ Century Anglo-Saxons, Vikings and Normans take turns to reign

But after 1066 England will never be conquered again

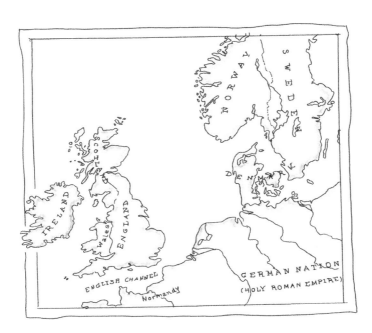

11th CENTURY (1001 to 1100)

English Monarchs

Ethelred II the Unready	978-1013	Anglo-Saxon
Sweyn Forkbeard	1013-14	Danish (Viking)
Ethelred II the Unready	1014-16	Anglo-Saxon (restored)
Edmund II Ironside	1016	Anglo-Saxon
Canute	1016-35	Danish (Viking)
Harold I Harefoot	1035-40	Danish (Viking)
Hardicanute	1040-42	Danish (Viking)
Edward the Confessor	1042-66	Anglo-Saxon
Harold II Godwinson	1066	Anglo-Saxon
William I the Conqueror	1066-87	Norman
William II Rufus	1087-1100	Norman
Henry I	1100-35	Norman

Scottish Monarchs

Kenneth III	997-1005	
Malcolm II	1005-34	
Duncan I	1034-40	Dunkeld
Macbeth	1040-57	
Lulach	1057-58	
Malcolm III	1058-93	Dunkeld
Donald III	1093-94	Dunkeld
Duncan II	1094	Dunkeld
Donald III	1094-97	Dunkeld (restored)
Edgar	1097-1107	Dunkeld

1028

King Canute tries to stop the sea

Really, are you kidding me?

1028: KING CANUTE

Curiously, the first event of this history may never have happened at all. But its legend is a famous part of British history, from the time it was first recorded in the 12th century by Henry of Huntingdon. The story goes that in 1028 King Canute had his throne set down by the seashore and commanded the tide not to come in. The tide came in nevertheless. This was said to be a demonstration by Canute to his flattering courtiers that he had no control over the elements, and that he was, like everyone else, subject to the greater power of God. The story is often wrongly told as an example of the arrogance of kings - with King Canute expecting his command to be obeyed.

An England, then populated largely by Anglo-Saxons, had been raided by Viking tribes from Norway, Denmark and Sweden from the year 793. Over the next 200 years the Vikings created settlements in England. By the late 800s they occupied a large part of Northern and Eastern England. This area became known as Danelaw. Following a full-scale invasion in 1013, Canute's father, the Danish king Sweyn Forkbeard, was crowned King of England. When Sweyn died the English crown passed to the Anglo-Saxon, Edmund Ironside of Wessex. So, Canute also had to win the throne of England by conquest, which he did in 1016. He added the throne of Denmark in 1018, and that of Norway in 1028. Together his kingdoms were called the Anglo-Scandinavian or North Sea Empire. Known as a very devout King, as the story of the waves demonstrates, Canute died in 1035, at the age of 40, in Shaftesbury in Dorset.

After Canute's death, his son, Harold Harefoot, was elected Regent as another son, Hardicanute, who had the better claim to the throne was stuck in Scandinavia. Harold betrayed his brother by making himself King in 1037. He died in 1040, and Hardicanute then became King.

1055

Edward the Confessor's new Abbey at Westminster is going to be more than first appears

Every king and queen of England will be crowned there for the next thousand years

1055: WESTMINSTER ABBEY

Edward the Confessor became King of England in 1042. He succeeded King Canute's son, Hardicanute, who was the last Viking king of England and also his half-brother. Edward was considered to be very religious and he was named as a saint by the Pope, a century later, in 1161. In 1055 Edward started rebuilding St Peter's Abbey, on the site of what is now Westminster Abbey, to provide himself with a burial church. The building was not completed until 1090, but it was used as a church from the end of 1065, just before Edward's death, in January 1066.

Edward died without children, and on his deathbed he named the earl Harold Godwinson as his successor. King Harold, as he became, and every king and queen of England subsequently, were crowned at the Westminster Abbey site. The only exceptions were Edward V and Edward VIII, who were never crowned. The coronation is a religious ceremony, reflecting the fact that rulers were considered to have been chosen by God and to derive their authority from God.

Work on building the present church of Westminster Abbey was begun by Henry III in 1245. But it was not completed until 1517. Further additions were also added later.

Edward the Confessor's Abbey was on a small island, next to the River Thames, known as Thorney Island. Due to building and earth works in the following centuries, it is no longer an island. The Abbey was first informally known as West Minster, because it was an important church (known as a minister) a little to the west of the old walled City of London. Soon the Abbey, and the entire area, was called Westminster. This included a royal palace which Edward built next to the Abbey site - between it and the Thames - which became the Palace of Westminster. While none of the original palace building survives, Westminster Hall, which forms part of the current Palace of Westminster, was built at the end of the 11th Century. The Palace of Westminster is now the location of the Houses of Parliament.

1066

Normans come to Hastings when claim to crown denied

William conquers in Battle, as Harold is de-eyed

1066: BATTLE OF HASTINGS

Harold's father, Godwin, had been made the Earl of Wessex by King Canute in 1018, and was a very powerful figure. He played an important role in securing the crown for Edward the Confessor, and when Edward died childless, in 1066, Edward named Godwin's son, Harold, as his successor. Harold immediately had to fight challengers for the throne. The first was Harold's own brother, Tostig, who supported an invasion of England by the Norwegian king, Harald Hardrada. They were both killed when King Harold's army defeated them at the Battle of Stamford Bridge in Yorkshire in September 1066.

Harold's army then had to march south to meet the second challenger, William, the Duke of Normandy. William was a cousin of Edward the Confessor and claimed that Edward had promised him the throne in 1051, and that Harold had sworn to support William's claim in 1064. William, with a force of as little as 7,000 men landed in the south of England, near to Hastings. He joined battle with Harold's army a few miles away on 14 October 1066.

Whilst Harold's army consisted almost entirely of foot soldiers, William's army had many cavalrymen and archers. The battle lasted throughout the day, but came to an end after Harold was killed when an arrow hit him in the eye.

There was relatively little further resistance, and William was crowned as King of England, at the site of what is now Westminster Abbey, on Christmas Day 1066.

1066 is considered to be the last time that England was ever conquered by a foreign invader. It kicked off a long period of Norman rule.

A few years after William's conquest, a famous 70 metre long embroidery was made, now known as the Bayeux Tapestry, which depicted the events up to and including the Battle of Hastings.

1085

The King wants taxes - and not to let anyone off the hook

It isn't just a great survey, it's the Domesday book

1085: DOMESDAY BOOK

In 1085 King William, who is usually known as William the Conqueror, ordered a comprehensive survey of most of the land and livestock in his English kingdom. The main purposes of the survey were to re-establish all of the rights of the Crown that had existed at the time of Edward the Confessor's death and to make easier the assessment and collection of land taxes and other monies due to the Crown.

The records of the survey were kept in a book, which later became known as the Domesday book from about 1221 onwards. There were two volumes, known as "Little Domesday" (which covered Norfolk, Suffolk and Essex) and "Great Domesday" (which covered most of the rest of England and some of Wales). Within these works a total of 13,418 places are named.

The King was considered to be the only true owner of the land and the right to hold any land at all therefore came from the King. The Domesday book listed the landholders and the size of the different pieces of land. It shows that the majority of the land in England at that time was held by people who had accompanied William from Normandy in 1066. Lords and Bishops and other senior members of the Church were the primary landholders, and others then held their land under them. At the bottom of the ladder were peasants (who were allowed to hold a small amount of land in return for working on the land of their lord), and serfs (slaves who owned no land).

Land was divided into "manors" of different sizes, and the value of each holding was recorded, together with the use of the land and the number of sheep, pigs and other livestock found there.

A number of towns and areas, including the City of London, Winchester and County Durham, which, by earlier charters, were not subject to taxation by the King, are not included in the Domesday Book.

1096

Exactly when Oxford University was founded is a matter of conjecture

But students in the reign of William the Second attended the first lecture

ALL SOULS COLLEGE OXFORD

1096: OXFORD UNIVERSITY FOUNDED

William Rufus succeeded his father, William the Conqueror, as King of England in 1087 –becoming King William II. It was during his reign that the first teaching occurred in Oxford, although the precise date when Oxford University was founded is unclear. Oxford University is the oldest university in the English-speaking world.

After Henry II stopped English students from attending the University of Paris in 1167, Oxford developed rapidly. In 1209, following violent conflict between its students and people living in Oxford, some of its academics fled to the town of Cambridge in the East of England and established Cambridge University. These two universities are considered among the best in the world.

Today, Oxford is made up of 39 self-governing colleges, the oldest of which, called University, Merton and Balliol, were established from 1249 onwards. These colleges developed out of halls of residence for students, which had been created as a result of further conflicts between students and townspeople in the first half of the 13th century.

Oxford was considered the pre-eminent seat of learning in Europe by 1350, and graduates of Oxford and Cambridge University have played a leading role in national life for the past 800 years. Part of this success was achieved by these universities persuading Edward III to block the creation of any further universities in England in 1334. Thereafter, no new universities were permitted in England until Durham University was founded in 1832. This also contributed to the success of Scottish universities, the earliest of which, St Andrews, was started 1410. The University of Edinburgh was founded in 1582.

1100

Henry the First's seizure of crown at Winchester is contested bitterly

Elder brother Robert has the better claim to the throne, but he is in Italy

1100: HENRY I

When William the Conqueror died, in 1087, he was survived by 3 of his 4 sons. His eldest, Robert, became the Duke of Normandy. However, William left his land in England to his third son, William Rufus, who became King William II. He gave money, but no land, to his fourth son, Henry. None of his sons were happy with this arrangement, and there followed conflict between them.

Henry was present when William II died in a hunting accident on 2nd August 1100 in the New Forest. Henry immediately went to Winchester Castle and seized the Royal Treasury. He claimed the throne of England ahead of his older brother Robert on basis that he was born in 1068, and that, unlike Robert, he had been born after William the Conqueror became King of England. Robert was at this time in Italy, returning from the First Crusade, which was an attempt, organised by the Pope, to capture Jerusalem and the Holy Land from non-Christians.

Henry was crowned at the Westminster Abbey site on 5th August 1100, and became King Henry I. However, when Robert returned to Normandy, he claimed that the English throne was rightfully his, and in 1101 he tried to invade England with his army. His attempt was unsuccessful, largely because of the lack of support from people in England. Robert was forced to renounce this claim and returned to Normandy.

Henry then invaded Normandy in 1105 and defeated and captured Robert at the battle of Tinchebray in 1106. Robert remained his prisoner for the rest of his life, and Normandy became a possession of the English crown.

12th CENTURY

In the 12th Century the fight for dominance of an Anglo-Norman empire rages

As feudal lords battle and revolt in the High Middle Ages

12th CENTURY (1101 to 1200)

English Monarchs

Henry I	1100-35	Norman
Stephen	1135-54	Blois
Henry II	1154-89	Plantagenet
Richard I the Lionheart	1189-99	Plantagenet
John	1199-1216	Plantagenet

Scottish Monarchs

Edgar	1097-1107	Dunkeld
Alexander I	1107-24	Dunkeld
David I	1124-53	Dunkeld
Malcolm IV	1153-65	Dunkeld
William I	1165-1214	Dunkeld

Lords and Monarchs of Ireland

Henry II made his son, John, Lord of Ireland in 1177. John retained this title when he became King of England in 1199. All subsequent Kings of England were also Lord of Ireland until King Henry VIII. In 1542 Henry VIII was given the new title of King of Ireland. Monarchs of England were thereafter also monarchs of Ireland until 1949. In that year much of Ireland became a republic, and only Northern Ireland remained part of the United Kingdom.

1135

King Stephen broke his oath and struggled to be a kingdom builder

But he survived the Anarchy and a civil war with Empress Matilda

1135: KING STEPHEN

Stephen of Blois was the son of William the Conqueror's daughter, Adela. Stephen nearly died together with King Henry I's son, who drowned in 1120 when the White Ship sank. After his son's death, Henry was left with only one legitimate child, his daughter, Matilda. Henry made the members of his court, including Stephen, swear an oath that they would support Matilda's succession to the Crown on his death. However, when Henry died in 1135, with the support of the English Church, Stephen seized the throne.

Matilda was known as Empress Matilda, because in 1114 she married Heinrich V, who was emperor of the Holy Roman Empire (which consisted of what is now Germany and other central European states). After Heinrich V died in 1125 Matilda married Geoffrey of Anjou in 1128.

In 1139, while her husband, Geoffrey, set about successfully conquering Normandy, Matilda sought to take the English throne by force. She captured King Stephen at the Battle of Lincoln in 1141, but failed to get herself crowned Queen of England. She agreed to free Stephen in exchange for the freedom of her half-brother, Robert. A civil war continued for a number of years, which was known as the Anarchy (due to the widespread lawlessness in the country).

By 1149 Matilda's forces were led by her son, Henry FitzEmpress. The civil war continued to ravage the country until 1153, when an agreement was reached between Stephen and Henry FitzEmpress, known as the Treaty of Winchester. Under this treaty Stephen was allowed to remain king until his death, but would be succeeded by Henry rather than Stephen's own son, Eustace. Stephen died in 1154, and Empress Matilda's son was crowned as King Henry II.

1154

*English Pope Adrian, the only ever
to appear*

*Was once a monk called Nicholas
Breakspear*

1154: ENGLISH POPE ADRIAN

Today there are many different Christian churches, with different practices and different ways of worshipping Jesus Christ. But for its first thousand years Christianity essentially had one Church – the Catholic Church. The word "catholic" means "universal", and Catholicism is still by far the largest Christian denomination. The leader of the Catholic Church is the Pope, who is considered by Catholics to have absolute authority, given by God, in matters of religion. The first Pope was one of Jesus's 12 disciples, St Peter – who is considered to be the founder of the Christian church. There is then a largely unbroken succession of Popes right up to the present day, with each Pope elected by senior churchmen, usually cardinals, following the death of the previous Pope.

There has only been one English Pope. This was Nicholas Breakspear, who selected the name Pope Adrian IV when he was elected as the Pope on 4th December 1154. He was the Pope until his death in 1159.

Nicholas was born in Bedmond in Hertfordshire in 1100. He was educated at the Abbey School in St Albans, but failed to be admitted as a monk at his local monastery. He therefore moved to France and became a monk at St Rufus monastery in southern France. He rose to the head of the monastery, and was elected as its abbot in about 1145. He came to the attention of then Pope, Eugene III, who made him a cardinal bishop in 1149. He worked as the Pope's representative in Scandinavia from 1152 to 1154, and was elected Pope in Rome on the death of Pope Anastasius IV.

As Pope, in 1155, he encouraged King Henry II to invade and take control of Ireland, in order to bring the Irish church under papal authority.

1170

Henry's rash words may not really have been intended

But 4 knights went to Canterbury and Becket's life ended

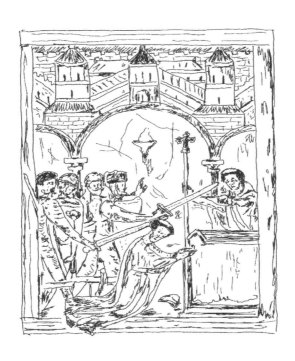

1170: THOMAS BECKET

The Archbishop of Canterbury was the most senior churchman of the Christian Church in England. The first such Archbishop, Augustine, had been sent by the Pope in 597. The Church was extremely powerful and wealthy in the Middle Ages, holding vast estates and privileges. Its position often brought it into conflict with Kings, who sought to assert their authority over it.

Thomas Becket was born in London in 1120. His father was a fairly wealthy merchant and property owner, and as a young adult Thomas secured a place in the household of the then Archbishop, Theobald of Bec. Under Theobald, Thomas studied church law and visited Rome on several occasions. Theobald made Thomas Archdeacon of Canterbury in 1154. He was so efficient in this and other posts that Theobald recommended Thomas to King Henry II for the post of Lord Chancellor. Henry gave Thomas this office of state in 1155.

Thomas' main role was to collect revenue and he worked extremely diligently for the King, becoming his close friend. Henry appointed Thomas as Archbishop of Canterbury in 1162. However, Thomas then earned Henry's displeasure by standing up for the rights of clergyman against the Crown. The difficulties between them became so great that Thomas fled from England in 1164, and lived in France in exile until 1170, when an agreement was reached allowing him to return.

But Thomas continued to anger the King with his actions, and Henry is reported to have said: "Will no one rid me of this turbulent priest". Four knights understood this as an order to kill Thomas, and on 29 December 1170 they travelled to Canterbury and murdered him in the Cathedral. Thomas was made a saint by the Pope in 1173, and Henry was forced to humble himself publicly before Becket's tomb.

1189

For good King Richard England
dearly paid

A lionhearted stranger who went on
a crusade

1189: RICHARD THE LIONHEART

In 1170 Henry II had his son, also called Henry, crowned as King of England and named Duke of Normandy. He also made other sons, Richard and Geoffrey, Duke of Aquitaine and Duke of Brittany. However, despite dividing up his territories in this fashion, Henry retained overall control, which led to his children rebelling against him. His son Richard earned the nickname "Lionheart" because of his prowess as a military commander during this period.

The younger Henry died before his father, and Richard became King of England after Henry II's death in 1189. Although Richard was born and raised in England, he lived most of his adult life in Aquitaine in France. While Richard the Lionheart has for centuries been regarded as an English hero, Richard largely used England as a source of income to fund foreign exploits. Upon taking the throne Richard focused on raising the vast sums required to enable him to go on the Third Crusade, to reconquer the Holy Land which was then occupied by Saladin, the Sultan of Egypt and Syria. After appointing trusted supporters to look after his various territories, Richard left for the crusade in 1190. The crusade succeeded in capturing the major cities of Accra and Jaffa, but failed in its primary aim to retake Jerusalem.

On Richard's return trip to England, in late 1192, he was captured by Leopold V, Duke of Austria, and then handed as a prisoner to the Holy Roman Emperor, Heinrich VI, who demanded a ransom of 100,000 pounds of silver for his release. The money was raised through further large taxation and Richard returned to England in 1194. Richard forgave his youngest brother, John, who had rebelled against him in his absence, and named John as his successor. Richard spent much of the rest of his life fighting in France, and was killed there by a crossbow arrow fired from a castle wall in 1199.

13th CENTURY

In the 13th Century we see the first steps to the people being empowered

And into a united kingdom Wales is devoured.

13th CENTURY (1201 to 1300)

English Monarchs

John	1199-1216	Plantagenet
Henry III	1216-72	Plantagenet

Monarchs of England and Wales (from 1283)

Edward I	1272-1307	Plantagenet

Scottish Monarchs

William I	1165-1214	Dunkeld
Alexander II	1214-49	Dunkeld
Alexander III	1249-86	Dunkeld
Margaret	1286-90	Sverre
No Monarch	1290-92	First Interregnum
John Balliol	1292-96	Balliol
No Monarch	1296-1306	Second Interregnum

1215

John signs Charter under pressure from barons at Runnymede

Fundamental rights of subjects by King guaranteed.

1215: MAGNA CARTA

When John succeeded his brother, Richard, as King of England in 1199, he also inherited land covering the whole western half of France – from the Duchies of Normandy and Brittany in the North right down to Aquitaine and Gascony in the South. However, as soon as he learned of Richard's death, the King of France, Philip Augustus, invaded Normandy and persuaded his allies in the rest of John's French territories to rebel. By 1204 John had lost all but a coastal part of Aquitaine. As a result, for the first time in 50 years, a king of England was now spending the majority of his time actually living in England. He became known as a cruel and ruthless king, as he sought to dominate all of his subjects and extract vast sums from them to support his foreign, and largely unsuccessful, wars.

The extreme financial demands he made on his barons and the Church earned the anger of both. In 1215, after another failed campaign in France, a group of barons renounced their loyalty to John and rebels took over the City of London. They demanded reform, and the end of the absolute power of the King to do whatever he wanted. John was forced to negotiate, and in June 1215, at Runnymede in Surrey, a treaty, known as the Magna Carta was agreed. The charter was mainly intended to protect the Church and the barons, and to limit the King's ability to imprison them or tax them, but some parts also extended to the general populace.

While the Magna Carta was renounced almost immediately by John, it lay the foundation for other charters to follow. When John died the following year, in 1216, his successor, King Henry III, resurrected the Charter in a revised form to try to gain the support of rebel barons. The Magna Carta is considered to be the start of constitutional government and the protection of rights and freedoms in law.

1233

North Eastern fortunes rise with England's first recorded mine

So, don't bother to carry coal to Newcastle upon Tyne

1233: FIRST COAL MINE

Although the Romans exploited the coalfields of northern England a thousand years earlier, the next record of a coal mine in England does not appear until about 1233, when coal mining began in Newcastle. The incredible value of coal was only then being reappreciated, its main uses at that time being in metal working and burning lime to create mortar for building. In the early years of Henry III's reign coal was being traded in North-East England and Scotland. It was known as "sea coal" as it was usually found around the coast. By 1228 it was being transported for use in London. The Domesday Book, in 1086, sought to list everything of value, but made no mention of coal. Yet by 1281 an enquiry found that Newcastle had doubled in value in just a few years, on account of its coal mines. By 1334 Newcastle was the fourth wealthiest town in England, after London, Bristol and York.

Early mines were known as bell pits, as they were created by digging straight down until a seam of coal was reached, and then outwards in the shape of a bell. All forms of mines were a source of great danger, not just from collapsing roofs but also from coal gas exploding – ignited by the candles used to light them. But the use of coal as a fuel was considered so valuable as to justify a huge toll of death and injury, as well as the noxious air pollution caused by burning it on a large scale.

Britain's industrial revolution, in the 18th century, was fuelled entirely by coal. Coal was used to power steam engines, and the steam engines in railways and steamships helped Britain to become the greatest world power in the 19th Century.

In the 20th Century coal was succeeded by oil as the dominant form of energy. But by the 21st Century all carbon-based fuels are being phased out in favour of non-polluting, environmentally friendly, alternatives.

1265

De Montford does not want his capture of King to be a crime

So calls people's representatives to Parliament for the first time

1265: FIRST PARLIAMENT

Henry III was only nine years old when he assumed the throne in 1216 on the death of his father, King John. His long reign, which lasted until 1272, was dominated by conflict with and between the barons. In order to secure the barons' support for further efforts to try to recapture land in France, Henry issued a new version of Magna Carta, known as the Great Charter, in 1225.

In 1258 rebel barons led by Roger Bigod and Simon de Montford forced Henry to agree to govern through a council of barons and churchmen. Parliaments, consisting of barons and delegations of knights from the counties, had been regularly called to gather from the 1230s to approve the raising of taxes. De Montford was in favour of even more radical reform, to limit the power of both the King and the leading barons. Following several years of civil war, De Montford captured Henry at the Battle of Lewes in 1264. For a short time, De Montford was the effective ruler, although he did so in the King's name.

In January 1265, in an effort to gain support for his government, De Montford called a new Parliament, summoning not just barons and knights but also two of the leading citizens, known as burgesses, from each of the major towns. This was the first vaguely representative Parliament, and the body of knights and burgesses became later known as the "commons". From this eventually developed the two Houses of Parliament, the barons and bishops attending the House of Lords and the rest of the people, the House of Commons. De Montford is regarded as the founder of the House of Commons.

De Montford's rule was short lived. In 1266 he was defeated by Henry's son, Prince Edward, at the battle of Evesham and killed. But Parliaments in Edward's subsequent reign were to follow the De Montford model.

1283

*When Prince Llywelyn's rebellion
went off the rails*

*Edward marched in and conquered
all of Wales*

1283: CONQUEST OF WALES

Llywelyn ap Gruffydd was the leading lord in Northern Wales, and in 1258 adopted the title of Prince of Wales. This was not initially accepted by the English Crown, which had sought to dominate Welsh lords and lands for centuries. However, during his brief ascendancy, in 1265, Simon de Montford accepted Llywelyn's right to rule in Wales in exchange for 20,000 pounds. Following de Montford's death, Llywelyn launched a successful military campaign and persuaded King Henry III to recognise his title in return for a tribute of 2,000 pounds a year.

When Edward I became King of England in 1272 Llywelyn ceased making the payments, and in 1275 he refused to formally acknowledge Edward as his overlord or come to Chester to pay homage to him. He was declared a rebel by Edward in 1276, and Edward invaded Wales with a large army the following year. Llywleyn was forced to give up most of his lands, but allowed to retain his title. In 1282 Llwelyn supported a revolt started by his brother, which was similarly crushed by Edward. But this time Edward went further, and, by the Statute of Rhuddlan, Wales became part of his English Kingdom.

Edward I engaged in an extensive scheme of castle building in Wales. His father, Henry III, had strategically placed castles in Cardigan, Carmarthen, Aberystwyth, Builth and Montgomery, and Edward followed these with castles in Harlech, Caernarfon and Conwy.

In order to consolidate his position in Wales, Edward arranged for his son, also called Edward, to be born at Caernarfon Castle in North Wales. In 1301 he gave his son the title of Prince of Wales. Since that time male heirs to the English throne have usually been invested with this title, and England and Wales have been a united kingdom for more than 700 years.

14TH CENTURY

In the 14th Century battles for
Scotland and France wage

A time of war and pestilence and
peoples' rage

14th CENTURY (1301 to 1400)

Monarchs of England and Wale

Edward I	1272-1307	Plantagenet
Edward II	1307-1327	Plantagenet
Edward III	1327-1377	Plantagenet
Richard II	1377-1399	Plantagenet
Henry IV	1399-1413	House of Lancaster

Scottish Monarchs

No Monarch	1296-1306	Second Interregnum
Robert I the Bruce	1306-1329	Bruce
David II	1329-1371	Bruce
Robert II	1371-1390	Stuart
Robert III	1390-1406	Stuart

1314

At Bannockburn the Scots let loose

Who beat England? Robert the Bruce

1314: BANNOCKBURN

King Edward I was given two famous nicknames. The first was Edward Longshanks, because he was very tall. The second was "Hammer of the Scots", earned through his crushing defeat of Scottish forces in 1296. Prior to this, in 1290, Edward had been asked by Scottish lords to help resolve a dispute over the Scottish crown. His price for assisting was an insistence that the Scots recognised his overlordship of Scotland. While John Balliol was chosen as the Scottish King in 1292, the Scots were never willing to submit to Edward and instead formed an alliance with France. As a result Edward invaded Scotland in 1296, deposed Balliol and imposed English control. The Scots rallied back under the leadership of William Wallace, who won a famous victory at Stirling Bridge, before losing to Edward at the battle of Falkirk in 1298. The conflict continued until Wallace was captured and executed by Edward in 1305, after most Scottish nobles had pledged allegiance to Edward.

But all was to change to 1306, when Robert the Bruce murdered his nearest rival and was crowned King of Scotland. He started a new campaign for Scottish independence. Edward responded with extreme savagery, but this did not quell the resistance. In 1307 Edward died and was succeeded by his son, Edward II. The new King lacked the ruthless leadership of his father, and Bruce was able to build forces against him.

In 1314 there was a major battle for control of Stirling castle, known as the battle of Bannockburn. Although the English Army considerably outnumbered the Scottish Army, Bruce was victorious. Edward was forced to flee, and Bruce followed this with raids into Northern England and also against English forces in Ireland. The Pope recognised Bruce as the King of an independent Scotland in 1324, and Edward III gave up all claims to Scotland in a treaty in 1328. Bruce died in 1329, the undisputed ruler of Scotland.

1327

*Ousted by son and wife, a kingdom
is transferred*

*And the second Edward is
succeeded by the third*

1327: EDWARD II DEPOSED

Edward II came to the throne in 1307 and was regarded as an incompetent king. For much of his reign he allowed a small number of favourites to exercise considerable power, in particular Piers Gaveston and the Despenser family. This was intensely disliked by many of the barons, leading to continuous conflict. In 1308 Edward travelled to France and married the 12 year old daughter of the King of France, Isabella. He had left Gaveston in charge of the kingdom while he was away, and on his return the barons insisted that Gaveston be exiled. Edward was forced to agree, but sent him to Dublin as Lord Lieutenant of Ireland. Gaveston returned in 1309, was exiled again in 1311, then returned again and was captured and executed by England's most powerful baron, the Earl of Lancaster, in 1312. Edward was furious but civil war was averted.

After the disaster of defeat to Robert the Bruce at Bannockburn in 1314, the Scots mounted a sustained assault on northern England, and England suffered a 7-year famine and serious revolts. Finally, civil war broke out in 1321, largely because of the barons' dislike of the power that Edward had given to the Despenser family. Edward succeeded, and was able to punish many of his opponents, including trying and executing the Earl of Lancaster for treason.

In 1326 Edward was required to pay homage to his brother in law, now the King of France, for his lands in Gascony. He made his son, also Edward, Duke of Gascony and sent him instead with Isabella. But in France Isabella formed a relationship with Roger Mortimer, an enemy of Edward during the civil war. Together they organised an invasion of England, with French assistance. They met little resistance, however. Mortimer took control. Edward was forced to abdicate in favour of his 14 year old son, who became Edward III, and was then murdered.

1337

*When claim to French throne denied
by no women law*

*The houses of Plantagenet and
Valois fight the hundred years war*

1337: THE HUNDRED YEARS WAR

Although Edward III was crowned as King in 1327, following the forced abdication of his father, his mother, Isabella, and her lover, Roger Mortimer, acted as regents and were the effective rulers for the first 4 years of his reign. But shortly before his 18th birthday Edward decided to take control, and had his mother and Mortimer seized at Nottingham Castle. Mortimer was accused of wrongly assuming royal power and, without trial, was hung at Tyburn. Edward was to reign for 50 years.

When Charles IV, the King of France, died in 1328, as his sister Isabella's son, Edward III was his closest living male relative. However, the French nobility rejected Edward's claim to the throne on the basis that no woman could claim the throne of France, and although Edward was male and the grandson of the French King Philip IV, his claim came through his mother. The French favoured the claim of Charles' cousin, Philip of Valois, who became King Philip VI.

Edward initially accepted the Valois claim, and even paid homage to Philip for his lands in France in 1329. But he changed his mind in 1337, when Philip seized the Duchy of Aquitaine. In 1340 Edward declared himself to be the true King of France. Thereafter, and for the next 116 years, English Kings lay claim to the kingdom of France and over this period fought numerous battles to try to put that claim into effect. This included famous English victories at Crecy in 1346, Poitiers in 1356 and Agincourt in 1415. Ultimately, however, the French were successful. Inspired by Joan of Arc, who in 1429 told the French Dauphin that God had told her to drive out the English, and who raised the morale of French troops at the siege of Orleans, the French started to win back territories. While Joan was captured and burned at the stake in 1431, the French resurgence continued. By 1453 England had lost all of its possessions in France except Calais, and the war was considered over.

1348

Black time for England, half the people die from disease

Blame the rats if you like, it was plague carrying flees

1348: BLACK DEATH

In 1346 Edward III defeated a large French army at the Battle of Crecy and a few weeks later his forces defeated the Scottish army at the Battle of Neville's Cross, capturing Scotland's King, David II. The following year he captured the important seaport of Calais, gaining a secure city in northern France for housing English troops, which would remain under English control until 1558. But he was unable to convert his advantage into ultimate victory, because the bubonic plague, later to be known as the Black Death, swept through Europe.

The plague was caused by a strain of bacteria carried by oriental rat fleas. Thought to have originated in central Asia, the Black Death arrived in south-east Europe in 1343. It travelled through the Mediterranean sea, as merchant ships were regularly infested with flea carrying rats, and across Europe. It is estimated to have killed up to 60% of the population of Europe.

In England, it arrived from Gascony in June 1348, reached London later that year, and by the summer of 1349 had covered the whole country, killing half of the people. Aside from the sheer terror created by whole communities dying rapidly, the social and economic consequences were profound. Farm labourers were suddenly in very short supply, and in an effort to try and keep wages from rising, Edward and his Parliament, consisting of all the great landholders, passed the Statute of Labourers in 1351. This created great resentment amongst the lower classes, but Edward was able to maintain order.

While the initial plague died down in 1350, it returned with vigour in 1361 and killed another fifth of the population. It continued to return intermittently over the next few centuries.

1381

The fight to end serfdom and high taxation was called the Peasants' Revolt

Wat Tyler's rebellion failed, but gave child King Richard a jolt

1381: PEASANTS' REVOLT

The population of England in 1348, before the Black Death arrived, was about 5 million. Within 3 years it had been reduced to just 2 and a half million people. The death toll was far higher amongst the poorer labouring class than it was amongst the local lords and landholding gentry, due to the conditions in which they lived. The majority of labourers worked on the land, and there still existed at that time a large number of serfs – a slave class, who were effectively owned by their lords. While the shortage of labourers, as a result of the plague, created opportunities for the lower classes to earn more and move into a greater range of occupations, laws were brought in by the landed class to try to restrict wages and movement. Resentment of this and the taxes levied on every person over the age of 14, to fund the war in France, were the primary causes of what was later known as the Peasants' Revolt, in 1381.

The revolt started in Essex, in response to the arrival of an unpopular tax collector, and quickly spread to Kent. Under the leadership of Wat Tyler, thousands of Kentish rebels marched on London. A 14-year-old King Richard II, who had succeeded his grandfather Edward III to the throne in 1377, had few troops available, as they were mostly engaged in France and the North of England. As the Tower of London was taken by the rebels, who killed the Lord Chancellor and many other lawmakers, Richard was forced to negotiate personally. He agreed to most of the rebels demands, including the abolition of serfdom.

When rebels demanded more, Wat Tyler was killed and Richard regained control. He revoked the charter he had agreed to, and revolts elsewhere across the country were suppressed. While this uprising had failed, Parliament was reluctant to impose taxes to support the French war thereafter. Serfdom disappeared in the following century.

1387

The tales of his Canterbury pilgrims could not have been coarser

But the father of English literature is Geoffrey Chaucer

1387: CHAUCER'S CANTERBURY TALES

Born in about 1346, the son of a wealthy wine merchant, Geoffrey Chaucer lived through the Black Death and the Peasant's Revolt, and fought in the Hundred Years war against the French. He served in the households of the Duke of Clarence and John of Gaunt, the Duke of Lancaster, and was in government service for three successive Kings. He was frequently involved in diplomatic work which took him across Europe on behalf of the King. As a servant of the King he was given a pension for life from 1367. When Richard II abolished Parliament in 1398 and became be an absolute ruler, his cousin Henry Bolingbroke, now the Duke of Lancaster, led an uprising in 1399 and deposed him, taking the crown as King Henry IV. However, Chaucer continued to be favoured by the new King just as he had been by the old.

But Chaucer's overwhelming claim to fame was as a poet in his own lifetime, and as the father of English literature in the following centuries. In the days before printing, when all books were hand written and had to be copied by hand, and most were written in French or Latin, Chaucer was a successful author, writing in what we now call Middle English.

His most important work was the Canterbury Tales started in about 1387. This consisted of 24 separate tales told by a group of pilgrims travelling together to visit the tomb of Saint Thomas Becket in Canterbury. The story tellers were from all walks of life, including a knight, a miller, a merchant and various people of the Church, and their stories are often funny and rude. They provide an entertaining insight into 14th Century England.

Chaucer died in 1400 and was buried in Westminster Abbey. His remains were moved, in 1556, to an area now known as Poets' Corner.

15th CENTURY

In the 15th Century Royal houses clash is followed by recovery

And knowledge can now be spread far and wide in the age of discovery

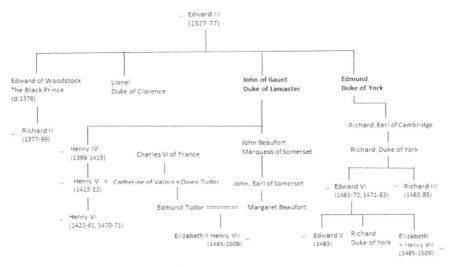

15th CENTURY (1401 to 1500)

Monarchs of England and Wales

Henry IV		1399-1413	House of Lancaster
Henry V		1413-1422	House of Lancaster
Henry VI		1422-1461	House of Lancaster
Edward IV		1461-1470	House of York
Henry VI	(restored)	1470-1471	House of Lancaster
Edward IV	(restored)	1471-1483	House of York
Edward V		1483	House of York
Richard III		1483-1485	House of York
Henry VII		1485-1509	Tudor

Scottish Monarchs

Robert III	1390-1406	Stuart
James I	1406-1437	Stuart
James II	1437-1460	Stuart
James III	1460-1488	Stuart
James IV	1488-1513	Stuart

1415

Outnumbered 4 to 1 by the French at Agincourt

Henry's longbows fill the breach and win the war

BATTLE OF AGINCOURT.

1415: BATTLE OF AGINCOURT

Richard II starved to death in captivity in 1400, less than 6 months after being deposed by Henry Bolingbroke, who had become King Henry IV. Richard II had left no legitimate children and had named one of his father's brothers, Edmund of Langley, the Duke of York, to be his successor. But Henry had the strongest claim to succeed Richard II, as he was the son of John of Gaunt, the Duke of Lancaster, who was an older brother of Edmund. He had to fight off a number of rebellions. He died in 1413, and his son become King Henry V.

Henry V is regarded as one the greatest warrior kings of England. This reputation is based in large part on his victory against the French in the Hundred Years War at the Battle of Agincourt in 1415.

Having persuaded Parliament and his Great Council to support a campaign in France to recover French territories, Henry V landed in Northern France in the summer of 1415 with about 12,000 men. By the Autumn, through war and disease, his army was down to about 9,000. It was this army that met the French army of some 36,000, near to the woods of Azincourt on 25 October. The decisive difference was that Henry had about 7,000 longbow men, and it was these archers who were able to devastate the French attack. The French lost many of their leading nobles in the battle, and Henry continued the campaign in 1417, eventually forcing the French into negotiations in 1420. These resulted in the Treaty of Troyes, in which Henry was named as the heir to French King Charles VI. Henry also married Charles' daughter, Catherine of Valois. But Henry never succeeded to the French throne, because he died in 1422, two months before Charles VI's death. Henry's 9 month old son, also Henry, was accordingly crowned King Henry VI of England and King Henry II of France. But the French throne was contested by his uncle, who became King Charles VII of France, and was finally considered lost in 1453.

1455

Lancaster roses are red, York roses are white

Crown swaps from one side to the other in 30 year fight

1455: WARS OF THE ROSES

The Wars of the Roses were named after symbols of the two opposing royal families - the house of York used an image of a white rose and the house of Lancaster was later identified by a red rose. John of Gaunt and Edmund of Langley were given the titles Duke of Lancaster and Duke of York by their father, King Edward III. The house of Lancaster first took the throne when John of Gaunt's son deposed Richard II, in 1399, and became King Henry IV. His son, Henry V, had a successful, but short reign, from 1413 to 1422. But his only child was less than a year old when he became King Henry VI, and during Henry VI's infancy and childhood the country fell into a state of considerable lawlessness, as the great nobles built up large private armies.

As an adult Henry VI was a weak king, dominated by ambitious lords. He lost the last of his French kingdom, apart from Calais, in 1453, and suffered a mental breakdown. Edmund of Langley's grandson, Richard, now Duke of York, supported by the powerful Earl of Warwick, ruled as regent. When Henry regained his senses in 1455, Richard sought to retain control, and the first battle between the two sides took place at St. Albans. Richard won, and continued as the Lord Protector. In 1459 the Lancastrian forces were temporarily able to restore Henry's direct rule. However, after Richard was killed in 1460, the Earl of Warwick, who became known as "the Kingmaker", helped Richard's son, Edward, the new Duke of York, to defeat Henry's army at the battle of Towton, and seize the throne, becoming King Edward IV in 1461.

By 1469 Warwick had fallen out with Edward, and warfare broke out between their forces. Warwick briefly restored Henry VI to the throne in 1470, but was defeated and killed by Edward's army in 1471. Henry VI was murdered, and Edward again reigned, until 1483. The Wars of the Roses were considered over with the first Tudor King, in 1485.

1477

*William Caxton's printing press
starts the revolution he planned
As Britain's first printed book beats
copying by hand*

1477: CAXTON'S FIRST PRINTED BOOK

The use of carved wooden blocks to create printed images originated in China at least 1,200 years before, and by 1400 block printing on paper had arrived in Europe, and was being used to print religious images and playing cards in volume. Movable type printing also originated in the far east. Small characters, carved out of wood, were pressed into clay to create a mould into which a tiny amount of molten metal was poured. When the metal was hard it could be coated with ink and used to print that character. In this fashion many letters of the alphabet were created in small metal pieces, which could then be arranged in blocks.

In 1439 Johannes Gutenberg from Germany started using this movable type technique in Europe, and by 1450 he had invented the printing press. By 1455 he had succeeded in printing the entire bible.

William Caxton was an English merchant born in Kent in about 1422. By 1453 he was living in Bruges, in what is now Belgium. Encouraged by the patronage of Margaret, Duchess of Burgundy, who was the sister of Edward IV, Caxton set up a printing press in Bruges, and printed the first book in English in 1473. He then returned to England and set up a press near to Westminster Abbey. The first book he printed there was an edition of Geoffrey Chaucer's *The Canterbury Tales* in 1477. He was to print more than 100 different books before his death in 1491, including classical stories and histories, many of which he translated himself from foreign texts.

Most of Caxton's printed books were in English, and he is credited with creating a standard English language through his printing. Until the 15th Century the language of the English royal court and between the nobility was French. Henry V had been the first English King to write in English, and the influx of Caxton's books, popular amongst the gentry, advanced reading and the use of English by all levels of society.

1483

The Princes' murder in the Tower remains a mystery

But Uncle Richard usurping the Crown –that's history

1483: PRINCES IN THE TOWER

After Edward IV had won back the crown in 1471, the remaining years of his reign were relatively peaceful. However, when Edward died suddenly in April 1483 his two sons, Edward and Richard, were aged 12 and 9. Edward became King Edward V, but his reign was to last only 78 days.

During his last illness, Edward IV had made a will naming his brother, Richard, Duke of Gloucester, as the protector of the realm while his son was still a child. However, after his death the majority of the nobles favoured instead the formation of a Council, with Gloucester as its president only. Gloucester moved rapidly to seize Edward V, executing those who opposed him, and putting the new king into the Tower of London. He was joined there a month later by his younger brother.

The Tower of London was traditionally the place where kings of England stayed while preparing for their coronation, and with his army in control of London, Gloucester was initially confirmed as the Lord Protector by the Council. However, a few days before Edward was due to be crowned, Gloucester's principal supporter, the Duke of Buckingham, went to the Guildhall and announced that both Edward and his brother were born out of wedlock, because when Edward IV had married their mother, Elizabeth Woodville, he was under contract to marry another. While almost certainly untrue, it meant that Richard of Gloucester could claim the crown. This was accepted by a Parliament, which he controlled, and on 26 June 1483 he became King Richard III.

The two princes, Edward and Richard, were never seen again after October 1483, and it was widely assumed that their uncle murdered them to secure his crown. Richard III was very unpopular as a result.

1485

Stanley's change of sides at Bosworth could not have been ruder

Richard the third was killed and we got Henry Tudor

1485: BATTLE OF BOSWORTH

After King Henry V's death in 1422, his widow, Catherine of Valois, secretly married one of her servants, a welsh courtier called Owen Tudor in about 1429. They had two sons, Edmund and Jasper. Henry VI became fond of his half-brothers and gave them titles. Edmund becoming the Earl of Richmond in 1449. Edmund married Margaret Beaufort, a great granddaughter of the first Duke of Lancaster, John of Gaunt, and their son, Henry Tudor, was born in Wales in 1457. While Henry Tudor's claim to the throne seemed very remote, after the murder of Henry VI in 1471, he was the most senior male Lancastrian still living, and he had to flee to Brittany in France.

With Richard III widely regarded as a usurper, and probable murderer of Edward V, a plot to replace him with Henry Tudor was started. After initial uprisings led by Richard III's former ally the Duke of Buckingham had failed, Henry Tudor promised to marry Edward V's elder sister, Elizabeth of York, and to unite the houses of Lancaster and York. When Richard III moved to marry his niece himself, Henry sailed from France with about 2,000 men, mostly French mercenaries, in August 1485.

Henry landed in Milton Haven, in his native Wales, and marched to England, his army growing along the way. Lacking experience in battle Henry gave command of his army to the Earl of Oxford. He met Richard and his army at Bosworth Field, near Shrewsbury, on 22 August 1485. Richard's army of about 10,000 men was twice the size of Henry's. However, Lord Stanley also brought 6,000 soldiers to the battlefield without declaring which side he was going to support. In the midst of the battle Richard saw that Henry was in a group separate from the fighting, and decided to lead a charge to try to kill him. He would have succeeded had Lord Stanley not intervened at that moment. Richard lost his horse and his head, and Henry claimed the crown by conquest.

16th CENTURY

The 16th Century is the time of Tudor Kings and Queens

Of Church and country, supreme rulers by any means

The Tudors

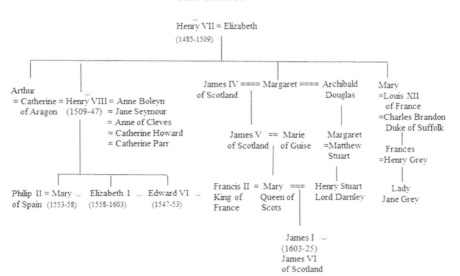

16th CENTURY (1501 to 1600)

Monarchs of England and Wales (and Ireland from 1542)

Henry VII	1485-1509	Tudor
Henry VIII	1509-1547	Tudor
Edward VI	1547-1553	Tudor
Lady Jane Grey	1553	Tudor
Mary I	1553-1558	Tudor
Elizabeth I	1558-1603	Tudor

Scottish Monarchs

James IV	1488-1513	Stuart
James V	1513-1542	Stuart
Mary I Queen of Scots	1542-1567	Stuart
James VI	1567-1625	Stuart

1509

Henry the Eighth rides onto the field and marries his dead brother's wife

He leaves with 6 brides down and a reformation of English life

1509: KING HENRY VIII

Five months after seizing the crown at Bosworth Field in 1485, Henry Tudor, now King Henry VII, married Edward IV's daughter, Elizabeth of York, thereby securing a much stronger royal pedigree for his sons than he himself enjoyed. Henry VII's reign was marked by caution, good administration, and a conciliatory approach to former enemies.

In 1509, Henry VIII came to the throne at the age of 17. His elder brother, Arthur, had died in 1502, at the age of 15, shortly after marrying Catherine of Aragon from Spain. The new King's first act was to marry his brother's widow, and they were crowned as King and Queen at Westminster Abbey in June 1509. Henry relished in the glory of kingship, spending extravagantly and embarking on foreign wars in his early years to try to win back the French crown. While he allowed his chief ministers, notably Cardinal Wolsey, Sir Thomas More and Thomas Cromwell extraordinary powers to govern his kingdom, he was absolutely ruthless towards those that fell out of his favour.

Catherine gave birth to Mary in 1516, but had no other children who survived infancy. Henry became obsessed with the idea of having a son to succeed him, and annulled his marriage with Catherine in 1533, so that he could marry Anne Boleyn. While Anne Boleyn gave him a daughter, Elizabeth, there was also no son, and Henry had her beheaded for alleged adultery in 1536. In the same year his Parliament passed the Second Succession Act, which declared Elizabeth, like Mary, to be illegitimate, and would have allowed Henry to name Henry Fitzroy, his illegitimate son, as his successor. But it was unnecessary as Henry's next wife, Jane Seymour, gave birth to the future Edward VI in 1537, but died 2 weeks later. Henry's marriages, to Anne of Cleves and Catherine Howard, both in 1540, ended in annulment and beheading. Catherine Parr, who he married in 1543, survived him. He died in 1547.

1533

Divorced from Catherine, Divorced from Rome

Watch your head when Henry's at home

THOMAS CROMWELL

1533: THE REFORMATION

While King Henry VIII was regarded as a well-educated and accomplished king, he was entirely merciless in asserting his absolute power. Shortly after his coronation he had two unpopular ministers of his father charged with high treason and executed, and throughout his reign the same fate befell many others. They were executed not because they opposed him, but because he decided that they had failed him in some fashion, or he saw some advantage in removing them.

Accordingly, when Cardinal Thomas Wolsey, who had been Henry's chief minister, and the effective ruler, from 1515 to 1529, failed to secure the Pope's agreement to the annulment of his marriage to Catherine of Aragon, he was stripped of his titles and charged with treason, but died before his trial. Henry declared himself to be the Supreme Head of the Church of England in 1531, and proceeded to remove all the powers of the Pope over the clergy in his kingdom. Anyone who refused to support him and take the Oath of Supremacy could be declared a traitor and executed. Such a fate met his Lord Chancellor after Wolsey, Sir Thomas More, in 1535. Thomas Cromwell, who as Henry's Principal Secretary from 1534 to 1540 was in effective control of the country, and who not only oversaw the split with the Pope and the Roman Catholic Church, but also the dissolution of the monasteries and sale of many rich Church estates to Henry's enormous financial advantage, failed Henry by persuading him to marry Anne of Cleves, whom Henry found repugnant, and was executed for treason.

While Henry's split with Rome occurred for very personal reasons, it was popular with many who supported the Reformation Protestant movement sweeping through Europe, started by Martin Luther in 1517. While Henry always considered himself a true Catholic, he started a religious conflict which would dominate national life for centuries.

1553

Lady Jane's nine day reign was for England quite contrary

A last hope to stop the Pope and a queen called Bloody Mary

IANA GRAYA

Regia stirps tristi cinxi diademate crines
Regna sed omnipotens hine meliora dedit

1553: LADY JANE GREY AND MARY

In 1543 Henry VIII's Parliament passed the Third Succession Act which restored both of his daughters, Mary and Elizabeth, to the line of succession, behind his son Edward. While Edward was 9 when he became King Edward VI in 1547, and only 15 when he died, he was nevertheless dedicated to the Protestant cause. Accordingly, as he was dying, he tried to prevent his half-sister, Mary, a devoted Catholic, from taking the throne by nominating his cousin, Lady Jane Grey, as his successor in his will. Jane was a committed Protestant and the granddaughter of Henry VIII's younger sister.

After Edward died, on 6 July 1553, Jane was proclaimed Queen on 10 July and started to prepare for her coronation. However, when Mary rallied her supporters, the Privy Council rapidly changed allegiance and declared Mary as Queen on 19 July. Mary had popular support and Parliament declared her the rightful Queen in September. Those who had supported Jane were executed for treason. Jane herself was spared for a few months, but was then executed in response to a Protestant rebellion organised by Thomas Wyatt, although she had no part in it.

Queen Mary's principal aim was to restore the country to Catholicism and to the supremacy of the Pope. In her short reign she was able to repeal recent religious laws and many Protestants were burned at the stake as heretics. Her persecution of Protestants led to her being called Bloody Mary. She married the Catholic Philip of Spain in 1554. While Philip was given the title King of England, he could only rule together with Mary. In 1556 Philip became King of Spain and was more interested in his lands across Europe.

Mary died childless in 1557, and was succeeded by her half-sister, who became Queen Elizabeth I. Elizabeth ended the return to Catholicism.

1587

Mother of the next English King, and Queen of Scots and of France in her day

Mary is held by cousin Elizabeth for 19 years then beheaded at Fotheringhay

1587: MARY QUEEN OF SCOTS KILLED

Henry VIII's elder sister, Margaret, was married to King James IV of Scotland in 1503. Their only child to reach adulthood ruled Scotland, as King James V, from 1513. His only legitimate child, Mary Stuart, was only 6 days old when he died in 1542 and she succeeded to the throne. Scotland was ruled by regents during her childhood. When Mary was just 6 months old, Henry VIII signed a treaty agreeing that she would marry his one-year old son Edward when she was 10 years old, uniting the crowns of England and Scotland when Edward became King. However, the Scottish Parliament rejected the treaty and Mary was then promised to Francis, the son of the French King. To keep Mary safe from English efforts to enforce the earlier treaty she was sent to live at the French court at the age of 5. She duly married Francis in 1558, and became the Queen of France in 1559. Francis died in 1560, and for the first time in 14 years Mary, now 19, returned to her Scottish kingdom.

She returned to a Scotland torn between Protestant and Catholic factions. She married her cousin Lord Darnley, and their son, James, was born in 1566. Darnley was murdered in 1567, and Mary then made herself extremely unpopular by marrying Lord Bothwell, the man generally thought to have murdered him. She faced an armed rebellion from her senior lords and was forced to abdicate her throne in favour of 1-year old James. She escaped from captivity and when a further effort to win back her crown was defeated, she fled to England. Mary hoped that the English Queen, Elizabeth, would help to restore her to her throne. However, Elizabeth was more concerned with the threat Mary posed to her own throne. Catholics considered that Elizabeth was illegitimate, and Mary was the true Queen of England. After holding her captive for 19 years, Elizabeth had Mary executed at Fotheringhay castle for treason. Mary's son, who had become James VI of Scotland on her abdication, was raised as a Protestant, and succeeded Elizabeth, becoming King James I of England.

1588

Spanish ships nearly burn in Calais,
England saved by Drake not Raleigh

1588: THE SPANISH ARMADA

When the English Catholic Queen, Mary, died in 1558 her half-sister, Elizabeth, who supported the Protestant reformation, took the crown. Mary's husband, King Phillip II of Spain, who until Mary's death had also enjoyed the title King of England and Ireland, saw Elizabeth as both illegitimate and a heretic. For many years he supported the cause of Mary Queen of Scots to become the English monarch. Concern about Spanish plots to overthrow her led Elizabeth to have Mary Queen of Scots executed in 1587. Elizabeth also encouraged piracy against Spanish ships returning from the Americas and aided a Dutch revolt against Spanish rule. In retaliation Philip decided to invade England and restore it to Catholicism.

In 1588 the Spanish Empire ruled by Phillip included Portugal, part of Italy, most of the Netherlands, large parts of South and Central America, and parts of Africa and Asia, including the Philippines, which were named after Philip. For his English invasion he amassed a fleet of 130 ships, carrying about 25,000 soldiers and sailors. The plan was to sail these to the Netherlands, where an army of a further 30,000 waited to be transported across the English Channel on barges.

An English fleet of 55 ships, commanded in part by Sir Francis Drake, harried the Spanish Armada as it sailed along the south coast of England. When the Spanish anchored for the night near Calais in a tight formation, Drake set alight 8 of his own ships and sailed them into the Spanish ships. While no Spanish ships were burnt, they had to scatter and out of formation were easier for the English to attack. They were forced north, and eventually sailed around the British Isles. Only 67 ships managed to return to Spain. Elizabeth famously rallied her forces at Tilbury, telling them "I have the body of a weak and feeble woman; but I have the heart and stomach of a king – and a King of England too". Victory over the Armada earned her the popular name Gloriana.nt

1591

It may be a Comedy of Errors on Shakespeare's first night

But the Globe will know no finer than Stratford's playwright

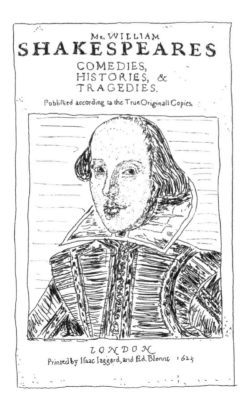

1591: WILLIAM SHAKESPEARE'S FIRST PLAY

William Shakespeare was born in the early part of Elizabeth I's reign, in Stratford-upon-Avon, in 1564. Relatively little is known about his private life. He was the son of John Shakespeare, who was a glovemaker and served as the mayor of Stratford in 1568. In 1582 he married Anne Hathaway, a farmer's daughter, who he was later to famously leave his second-best bed in his Will. Together they had 3 children. But Shakespeare was to find success in London, as an actor and writer of plays and poems, from about 1585.

Shakespeare is credited with at least 38 plays. Many of these were histories, including 3 about Henry IV, entitled *Henry IV Part I, Part II* and *Part III*, which may have been his first 3 plays to be performed, from about 1589. Other history plays included *King John, Richard III* and *Henry V*. He also wrote comedies, such as *The Comedy of Errors*, which some contend was his first play, and tragedies such as *Romeo and Juliet.* His other famous works included *A Midsummer Night's Dream, The Merchant of Venice, Hamlet, Macbeth and King Lear*.

Many of Shakespeare's plays were performed by a company of players called the Lord Chamberlain's Men. This company, of which Shakespeare was to own a share, was permitted to change its name to the King's Men after King James I took the throne in 1603, due to the popularity of the plays in the royal court. In 1599 Shakespeare's company built its own theatre on the south side of the River Thames, known as The Globe, due to its round shape.

When Shakespeare died in 1616, he was wealthy and famous. But this was as nothing to the fame that was to follow, as his plays were published in many editions and performed everywhere over the next four centuries. He is regarded as the world's greatest playwright.

17th CENTURY

In the 17th Century the House of Stuart meets its match in civil revolution

As struggles with the gentry in Parliament reach a glorious resolution

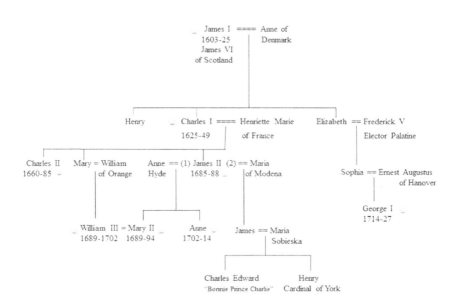

17th CENTURY (1601 to 1700)

Monarchs of England, Ireland and Wales

Elizabeth I   1558-1603   Tudor

Scottish Monarchs

James VI   1567-1625   Stuart

Monarchs of England, Ireland, Scotland and Wales

James I (VI in Scotland)   1603-1625   Stuart
Charles I   1625-1649   Stuart

Lord Protectors of The Commonwealth

Oliver Cromwell   1653-1658
Richard Cromwell   1658-1659

Monarchs of England, Ireland, Scotland and Wales

Charles II   1660-1685   Stuart
James II (VII in Scotland)   1685-1688   Stuart
Mary II (with William III)   1689-1694   Stuart
William III   1689-1702   Orange

1603

When Elizabeth dies without an heir of her own

James the sixth of Scotland takes the English throne

James I

1603: JAMES I

Queen Elizabeth I was known as the Virgin Queen, and, as the name implies, was never married and was childless when she died in 1603, after a reign of 45 years. She was the last of the Tudor monarchs, who had reigned since her grandfather, Henry VII, had seized the crown in 1485. She was succeeded by a great great grandchild of Henry VII, James Stuart, who had been the King of Scotland since the forced abdication of his mother, Mary Queen of Scots, in 1567, when he was only 1 years old. King James VI of Scotland then became King James I of England and Ireland.

The Scottish House of Stuart originated from the title High Stewart of Scotland given to Walter FitzAlan by Scottish King David I, in about 1150. His descendants adopted Stewart as their surname. The first member of the Stewart clan to become King of Scotland was Robert II, in 1371. Mary, Queen of Scots adopted the French spelling, Stuart, as she was brought up in France.

Although James had the clearest claim to succeed Elizabeth, Elizabeth never acknowledged this, and in her last years her chief minister, Robert Cecil, was forced to conduct a secret negotiation with James in an effort to secure a smooth succession. James was declared King of England on the day Elizabeth died. Unlike his mother, who had been a Catholic, James was raised in the Protestant Church of Scotland, and he encountered considerable celebrations as he journeyed from Edinburgh to London for his coronation at Westminster Abbey in July 1603. He reigned until 1625, but only returned to Scotland once – in 1617.

While James called himself King of Great Britain and Ireland, he actually ruled three separate kingdoms, each with its own Parliament and legal system.

1605

*He failed to blow up the King you
will remember*

*But it's still Guy Fawkes night on
the fifth of November*

1605: THE GUNPOWDER PLOT

When James I succeeded to the English crown in 1603, he indicated that he did not intend to persecute Catholics provided they obeyed the law. However as Catholic plots were uncovered his attitude hardened and in 1604 he ordered all Catholic priests to leave the country and reintroduced the collection of heavy fines for people who refused to attend Protestant worship services. The leading Catholic plotter, Robert Catesby, who in 1603 had been part of a group trying to persuade King Philip III of Spain to invade England in order to restore Catholicism, hatched a plot to kill James I and leading Protestant nobles and bishops by blowing up the Houses of Parliament at its State Opening.

Catesby and his fellow conspirators were able to rent a large storage cellar which was directly under the Parliament building. Into this cellar they placed 36 barrels of gunpowder - enough explosive power to completely destroy the building and kill everyone in it. The man chosen to light the fuse was a Yorkshireman called Guy Fawkes. Fawkes had been recruited as an experienced soldier who had fought for the King of Spain's army for a number of years. The scheme was to replace James I with his 9-year-old daughter, Princess Elizabeth

The gunpowder plot was discovered when an anonymous letter was sent to a Catholic nobleman warning him not to attend the State Opening. The letter was brought to the King, who ordered a thorough search, and Fawkes was discovered in the cellar with the barrels of gunpowder, and the means to ignite them, the night before the Opening on 5th November 1605. Under torture Fawkes revealed the names of other conspirators, who, like him, were then executed or killed. James I's narrow escape has been celebrated on 5th November ever since, initially with special annual services, and then with bonfires and fireworks. Guy Fawkes is traditionally burned in effigy on this night.

1611

King James' bible is the best translation yet

And for Christians and English a standard is set

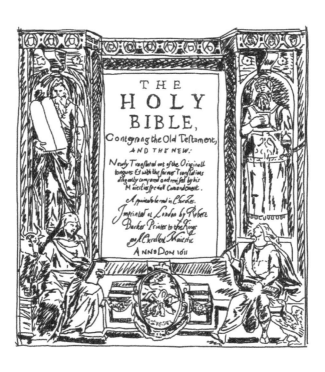

1611: KING JAMES BIBLE

One of the principal aims of the Protestant reformation was to make the Bible available in a language that ordinary people could understand. Traditionally the Bible was written in Latin, and most Christians had to rely on their priest to explain to them what it said. When Henry VIII founded the Church of England he ordered the production of an English translation of Holy Scripture, not only to be read from during Church services, but which could be read without the help of a clergyman. Elizabeth I ordered a further English translation, but the most famous was that ordered by King James I in 1604 shortly after he succeeded to the throne. First published in 1611, this later became known as the King James Bible, or the Authorised Version, and, due to its widespread use and popularity in the English speaking world ever since, is considered the most influential book in the English language.

The King James Bible contains 39 books of the Old Testament, translated mostly from Hebrew, and 27 books of the New Testament translated from Greek. These books, originally written by a number of ancient authors, were considered to be directly inspired by God, and therefore Holy Scripture. The original version of the King James Bible also included a third section, containing another 14 books, called the Apocrypha. These books were not considered to be Holy Scripture and were removed from later editions.

Some of the language of the King James Bible was considered old fashioned, even when it was first written, for example using "-th" rather than "-s", as in "hath" rather than "has" and "liveth" rather than "lives". While this has given scriptural language a distinctly recognisable style and sound, in general, the fact that the King James Bible was the most widely available and read book in English produced a standard English language in the succeeding centuries.

1620

Puritan pilgrims sail from Plymouth to America in the Mayflower

The birth of a nation who give thanks for food in their first hour

1620: THE MAYFLOWER

The Italian Christopher Columbus' discovery of the Americas, in 1492, opened up a New World of opportunity for the European powers. The Spanish and Portuguese were quick to capitalise on this, rapidly creating empires over the whole of South and Central America. England was to focus its efforts on North America, with Elizabethan, Sir Walter Raleigh, creating a short-lived colony in what is now North Carolina in 1585, before a permanent settlement was established, at Jamestown in Virginia from 1607.

A Puritan religious movement initially called the Brownists, after its leader Robert Browne, who led it from 1581, sought a separation from the Church of England, and as a result suffered persecution. A group, who became known as the Pilgrims, decided to create a colony in North America where they would be able to govern themselves and practice their religion freely, while remaining loyal to King James I. They set sail on board an old merchant ship called the Mayflower from Plymouth in September 1620 and landed in what they called New Plymouth, in what is now Massachusetts, in December 1620.

The settlement struggled through its first winter, with nearly half of the 102 settlers dying. They were able to establish friendly relations with the local Indian tribe, and in October 1621 they celebrated a harvest feast with them, which included wild turkey. This was later to be called the First Thanksgiving, and Thanksgiving is now a national annual holiday in the United States of America in late November.

The self-rule of the Plymouth colony did not last long, and as new English settlements were established along the eastern coast of North America, it became part of the Dominion of New England and eventually merged with the Massachusetts Bay Colony.

1642

*King and Parliament on top in turns
in Civil War mess*

*But after 7 years of fighting Charles
is ahead less*

1640: ENGLISH CIVIL WAR

Charles I came to the thrones of England, Scotland and Ireland on his father, James I's, death in 1625. He believed in the divine right of kings, and resented any attempt by Parliament to curtail his power. He therefore attempted to rule without Parliament, but could not do so because he was reliant on the cooperation of the gentry to collect taxes, and it was now long established that taxes would only be levied with their consent, given through Parliament. Nevertheless, he ruled without a Parliament from 1629 to 1640. Then a Scottish rebellion and financial necessity forced him to call a Parliament, to become known as the Long Parliament. This Parliament was dominated by Puritans and it sought not only force Charles to accept Parliaments must be called at least every 3 years and must give consent to taxation, but also to reform religion even further away from Catholicism.

The country became divided between areas supporting the Parliament, consisting mainly of the cities, and those supporting the King. Civil War broke out in 1642 after Charles unsuccessfully attempted to arrest 5 members of the House of Commons for treason. The Royalist armies, known as Cavaliers, initially enjoyed success against the Parliament's armies, known as Roundheads. But when Parliament re-organised its forces into the highly disciplined New Model Army, they crushed the Royalists at Naseby in June 1645. Charles was imprisoned in 1646 and the war briefly ended.

The Civil War broke out again in 1648, with Royalist uprisings and a Scottish invasion in support of the King. These were defeated by Parliamentarian troops, now led by Oliver Cromwell. Part of the Army, led by Thomas Pride, then forced out Parliamentarians who were still willing to have Charles as King. A Rump Parliament then found Charles guilty of treason as a public enemy. He was beheaded in January 1649.

1660

*Cromwell ruled as Lord Protector
when the Crown was spurned*

*Then Charles the second was
invited back and monarchy returned*

1660: RESTORATION OF MONARCHY

Oliver Cromwell was a member of Parliament for Cambridge at the start of the Civil War in 1642, and as a member of the Rump Parliament in 1649 signed Charles I's death warrant and then joined the Council of State responsible for the government of the newly declared Commonwealth of England. Having distinguished himself as a military commander for the Parliament in the civil war, Cromwell led a force into Ireland in order to crush Royalist forces seen as a threat to the Commonwealth, a campaign notable for the massacres of Irish Catholics. While the conquest of Ireland was completed in 1653, Cromwell had already moved onto Scotland by 1650, as the Scots declared Charles I's son as King Charles II of Scotland. In 1651 Charles II led a Scottish Army towards London, but was defeated by Cromwell at the Battle of Worcester and escaped to exile in France. The Commonwealth now controlled England, Ireland and Scotland.

In the face of disagreements as to the form of government that should be adopted, Cromwell accepted the title of Lord Protector in December 1653. He thereafter exercised the powers of a monarch, but when Parliament offered him the crown, in 1657, he refused it. He re-established the House of Lords, and nominated his son Richard as his successor as Lord Protector.

When Cromwell died, in 1658, Richard became Lord Protector, but lacking support in the Army or Parliament was forced to resign in 1659, bringing the Protectorate to an end. In the disarray that followed the Governor of Scotland, George Monck, led the Army into London and restored the Long Parliament. There then followed a general election, and, after Charles agreed to pardon those who fought against his father, the new Parliament invited him to return as king in 1660. He was crowned as King Charles II at Westminster Abbey in 1661.

1665

One in four die as London suffers a great loss

And bubonic plague houses are marked with a cross

1665: GREAT PLAGUE

While death from other diseases, such as smallpox and measles, was a common feature of 17th century life, the bubonic plague, spread by rat flees, since the Black Death in 1349, had never completely disappeared. From time to time major outbreaks had occurred over the next few centuries. The last of these occurred, principally in London, in 1665. This became known as the Great Plague of London, and over a period of 18 months killed about 100,000 people, a quarter of the City's population.

In 1665 12 times more people lived in and around London than in Norwich, which was the next largest English city. The majority of these were crammed into tightly packed slums both inside and outside of the City walls. These overcrowded areas stank, not only of the pollution from different industries and the coal burning to heat houses, but of raw sewage, which ran down the streets in open sewers. It was an easy breeding ground for disease, and the majority of the deaths occurred in these areas. At that time persons known as Searchers were employed to inspect corpses and determine the cause of death. If someone in a household was found to have died from the plague, no one else was allowed to leave the property for 40 days, often condemning all occupants to death. These houses were guarded and marked with a red cross on the door.

Charles II and his court, and many of the gentry, fled the City to avoid catching the plague. Charles moved his Court to Salisbury and then Oxford. He returned to London in early 1666, when the death toll had dropped significantly. Parliament was able to sit again in September 1666. Other cities were also badly affected by the plague, but a large part of the country managed to escape it due to the extreme quarantine measures that were adopted.

1666

Great fire started by spark in bakery in Pudding Lane

Only 8 dead and London rebuilt again

1666: GREAT FIRE OF LONDON

In the early morning of 2nd September 1666, a fire broke out in a bakery on Pudding Lane in the City of London. It was to burn for 5 days and to destroy more than13,000 houses, 89 churches, including the old Gothic style St. Paul's Cathedral, and the major administrative buildings of the City. While the fire ravished the commercial quarter of the City and the residences of the gentry in the centre of London, the outer, densely overcrowded, slum districts were relatively unscathed. For this reason, the death toll was very small, estimated at only 6 to 8 people

London at that time was very used to dealing with fires, which occurred frequently. With its narrow winding streets, and many timbered houses which were often 6 stories tall and grew outwards on the upper floors, so that they nearly touched the houses across the street, the City was an obvious fire hazard. A thousand people were employed to watch the streets at night, so that fires were spotted early. Every Church was required to store equipment for firefighting, including ladders, buckets and firehooks. Water was available through a system of pipes or could be passed up in buckets from the River Thames. The primary method of stopping a larger fire was to demolish the buildings around it, by pulling them down with the firehooks, or sometimes blowing them up with gunpowder. This created a firebreak and contained the fire.

Unfortunately, on that day, the Lord Mayor of London was too slow to give the order to demolish properties and create firebreaks. When the order did come it was from King Charles II himself, who had sailed down the Thames from his palace at Whitehall to view the fire. It was by then too late to avoid major destruction, and the fire spread rapidly across the City over the succeeding 3 days, eventually burning itself out when the wind dropped. Samuel Pepys gave graphic accounts of both the Great Plague and Great Fire of London in his famous diaries.

1687

Sir Isaac Newton lays down the laws

And no motion occurs without a cause

Isaacus Newton Eq Aur.

1687: SIR ISAAC NEWTON

In July 1687 Isaac Newton, a farmer's son who would become Britain's most famous mathematician and scientist, published his most famous work. At that time physical science was known as "natural philosophy", and his book was entitled "Mathematical Principles of Natural Philosophy" and was best known by the Latin word for first principles, *Principia.*

In this book Newton set out what he called the 3 laws of motion, which we now call the universal laws of motion. These are, firstly, that something only moves, or changes its motion, if force is applied to it; secondly that the change is directly proportional to that force; and thirdly, when two objects contact one another they apply an equal and opposite force against each other. The book contained other important advances in mathematics, and analysed mathematically the motion of all kind of bodies, including the planets in the solar system. The last part of the work described the principles of gravity in great detail. Famously, Newton stated that his inspiration to work out the laws of gravity came as a result of watching an apple fall from a tree in a garden in 1666.

The importance of Newton's work was recognised in his lifetime. At that time, it was a requirement that all senior academics, known as fellows, at Cambridge University had to be ordained into the priesthood of the Church of England. King Charles II granted Newton a special dispensation exempting him from this requirement. While Newton was a deeply religious man, a number of his religious beliefs were at odds with the Church. Newton served as a member of Parliament, and from 1696 was Master of the Royal Mint, responsible for the coinage of the realm. In 1703 he was made President of the Royal Society, and in 1705 he was knighted by Queen Anne. He died aged 84 in 1727. There is a monument celebrating him in Westminster Abbey, where he is buried.

1688

When James the Second tries to resurrect Catholicism the people are not keen

A glorious revolution makes nephew William King and daughter Mary Queen

1688: GLORIOUS REVOLUTION

Charles II converted to Catholicism on his death bed in 1685. Leaving no legitimate children, he was succeeded by his younger brother, who became King James II of England and Ireland and King James VII of Scotland. James had become a Catholic when he was 35, in 1668, and was to be last Catholic monarch. James, who was made Duke of York at birth, and after whom New York in America was named in 1664, never expected to become king. Charles II had insisted that James' two daughters, Mary and Anne, be raised in the Church of England. The older of these, Mary, married the Dutch leader, William of Orange, who was the nephew of Charles and James, and also a Protestant.

The Test Acts of 1673 and 1678, had excluded Catholics from all positions, but exemption had been made for James. Initially, James was well received as King, however opposition quickly grew as he sought to repeal the Test Acts by only permitting candidates who would support a repeal to stand for Parliament and he put Catholics in positions of power in the Army. There was a movement to replace James with William of Orange, which intensified when James had a son in June 1688, also called James, and therefore an heir who was likely to also be Catholic. William was invited to invade by English nobles. With assurances of support from English Protestants, William put together a force of about 15,000 and landed in England in November 1688. In the face of popular support for William, anti-Catholic rioting in cities and wholesale desertions from his Army, James capitulated and fled to France. A special Convention Parliament was elected, in January 1689, which resolved that James had abdicated leaving the throne vacant, and appointed William and Mary as joint monarchs of England. Scotland quickly followed, but largely Catholic Ireland continued to support James, and William had to defeat him at the Battle of the Boyne in 1690. The so-called Glorious Revolution was completed in 1691.

1689

With the Bill of Rights, cruel and unusual punishments are no more

And Parliament's consent is needed for new taxes or law

The BILL of RIGHTS ratified at the Revolution by King William, and Queen Mary previous to their Coronation

1689: BILL OF RIGHTS

William and Mary accepted the invitation of the Convention Parliament to be joint monarchs in early 1689 and were crowned as King William III and Queen Mary II at Westminster Abbey on 11 April 1689. The coronation oath that they swore, for the first time, included the promise to govern "according to the statutes in parliament agreed upon". The principle was established that the monarch could only govern with the consent of their subjects, expressed through Parliament. While only a privileged few were then eligible to vote for members of the House of Commons, this was nevertheless an important milestone on the road to a democratic government.

Parliament drew up a Declaration of Rights, which, with the assent of the monarchs, was enacted as the Bill of Rights in December 1689. This Act barred Catholics from the throne of England, and established important rights and liberties. In particular the Crown could not make or suspend laws without the consent of Parliament, could only levy taxes granted by Parliament, and could only keep a standing army in England with the consent of Parliament. It also declared that elections to Parliament should be free, and that members of Parliament enjoyed complete freedom of speech in their debates and could not be subject to any punishment for anything said there. The Act also provided that no one could be subjected to excessive fines or "cruel and unusual punishments".

In April 1689 a Convention of Scottish Estates voted to remove James as their King and offered the Scottish crown to William and Mary, who duly accepted. They also passed the Claim of Right Act, which served a similar purpose to the Bill of Rights in England.

1694

Bank of England established privately to raise money for new navy following French war

Helps Britain become dominant global power and a quarter of the World to have a common language and law

1694: BANK OF ENGLAND ESTABLISHED

Before William of Orange accepted the invitation to invade England and become its King, he was deeply concerned by the threat posed by Catholic France to the Protestant Dutch Republic. When he secured the English throne with his wife Mary, and James II fled to France, he secured the support of Parliament to join a Grand Alliance of Protestant European powers in a war against France, which became known as the Nine-Years' War. William was to spend much of his time away from England fighting, and until she died of smallpox in December 1694, Mary governed alone during these periods. After her death William continued to rule as a sole monarch until 1702.

By 1694 William was in desperate need to build up the English navy, following serious losses to the French, but his government lacked the funds to do so. He invited lenders to loan his government £1.2 million and those that did so were incorporated as The Governor and Company of the Bank of England, and granted considerable privileges including the right to issue banknotes. The money was raised in just 12 days. The navy was not only rebuilt, but soon became the most powerful in the world, and within a century Britain was the dominant global power.

The Bank of England, which was to move to Threadneedle Street in 1734, started with just 19 staff. It was created by a Royal Charter granted by William and Mary, who were also two of the original subscribers, to "promote the good and benefit of our people". While it was the depository of government funds and became the central bank of the United Kingdom, controlling the overall supply of money, it remained as a private bank until 1946, when it was nationalised.

The Bank of England became a model for other central banks in nations around the world.

18th CENTURY

In the 18th Century Scotland and Ireland decide to join United Kingdom at beginning and end

And government by Prime Minister and Cabinet is the Georgian trend

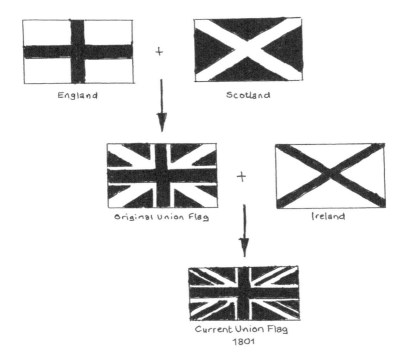

England   +   Scotland

Original Union Flag   +   Ireland

Current Union Flag
1801

18th CENTURY (1701 to 1800)

Monarchs of England, Ireland, Scotland and Wales

William III	1689-1702	Orange
Anne	1702-1714	Stuart

Monarchs of Great Britain and Ireland

Anne	1707-1714	Stuart
George I	1714-1727	Hanover
George II	1727-1760	Hanover
George III	1760-1820	Hanover

Prime Ministers of Great Britain

Sir Robert Walpole	1721-1742	Whig
Earl of Wilmington	1742-1743	Whig
Henry Pelham	1743-1754	Whig
Duke of Newcastle	1754-1756	Whig
Duke of Devonshire	1756-1757	Whig
Duke of Newcastle	1757-1762	Whig
Earl of Bute	1762-1763	Tory
George Grenville	1763-1765	Whig
Marquess of Rockingham	1765-1766	Whig
Earl of Chatham	1766-1768	Whig
Duke of Grafton	1768-1770	Whig
Lord North	1770-1782	Tory
Marquess of Rockingham	1782	Whig
Earl of Shelburne	1782-1783	Whig
Duke of Portland	1783	Whig
William Pitt the Younger	1783-1801	Tory

1707

Scotland's ruinous colony attempt could have been cannier

But saved by union with England, rule Britannia

1707: ACTS OF UNION – ENGLAND AND SCOTLAND

Queen Mary II died childless in 1694 and when her husband and co-monarch, King William III, also died, in 1702, he was succeeded by Mary's sister, Anne. Anne became the queen of 3 separate kingdoms, England, Scotland and Ireland.

There had been efforts to unite the kingdoms of England and Scotland since Anne's Great-grandfather, James, became king of both countries in 1603. There had been a short period during the Commonwealth, from 1657 to 1660, when England, Scotland and Ireland shared a single Parliament in Westminster. But this had proven unpopular and when the monarchy was restored with Charles II in 1660, it was disbanded. But efforts continued. Scottish leaders recognised that considerable economic benefits would follow from a political union, in particular that they would be able to trade freely with England and its colonies. There were however continuing objections based on religious differences.

In the 1690s Scotland suffered from an economic crisis and a severe famine, as a result of failed harvests, resulting in the death of about a tenth of the population from starvation. In 1698 a Scottish colony was established in Panama in Central America, but it was destroyed by the Spanish two years later. This led to financial ruin for investors in the project across Scotland. While a union with England remained unpopular with many Scots, their leaders sought to put pressure on the English parliament by passing the Act of Security in 1704, which would have meant Scotland having a different monarch to England after Anne's death. A Treaty of Union was negotiated and agreed in 1706, followed by Acts of Union passed by both parliaments, which guaranteed that Scottish law and courts would be maintained, and created the kingdom of Great Britain with one parliament. England also agreed to pay Scots investors for their losses in the Panama debacle.

1711

*For 250 years nothing in London
will be as tall*

*After Sir Christopher Wren rebuilt
the Cathedral of St Paul*

1711: SAINT PAUL'S CATHEDRAL

To commemorate the Great Fire of London, Charles II ordered the construction of a huge stone column close to Pudding Lane. Completed in 1677, it was 202 feet tall, with an internal spiral staircase and a viewing platform near the top, and it became known simply as the Monument. It originally carried an inscription at its base blaming Catholics for the fire, which was removed in 1830.

After the fire, there were initially ambitious plans for rebuilding the City of London in a grand style. However, these plans were abandoned due to lack of finance and the necessary labour. Instead the City was rebuilt on the old road layout, but with wider lanes and properties built of brick and stone rather than wood. Sir Christopher Wren, who was born in Wiltshire in 1632, and was already recognised for many scientific achievements, oversaw a lot of the works following his appointment as the King's Surveyor of Works in 1669. Wren, now considered one of world's greatest architects, helped to design, not only the Monument, but 52 of the churches that were rebuilt in the City, including the new St Paul's Cathedral on Ludgate Hill.

Work on St. Pauls, noted for its magnificent dome, commenced in 1669, and was declared complete in Queen Anne's reign in 1711. Wren, who was also a founder and president of the Royal Society, and designed many other notable buildings, was able to oversee the entire construction, and lived until 1723.

The Cathedral was to be a dominant presence in London for centuries, and at 365 feet tall, was the tallest building in London until the construction of Millbank Tower in 1963. It serves as the cathedral of the Bishop of London, and, together with Westminster Abbey, is used for religious services of national importance.

1714

George of Hanover was made King when Anne died

As 56 Catholics have to stand aside

1714: GEORGE I

Queen Anne died in 1714. Although she gave birth many times, none of Anne's children survived childhood, or her, and like 7 of the 9 monarchs that immediately preceded her, she was unable to pass the throne to her own child on her death. She was the last monarch of the house of Stuart.

Anne's deposed father, James II, had died in 1701, and his son, also called James, whose birth had precipitated his father's removal, had, as feared, been raised as a Catholic in exile in France. The problem of the succession after Anne had already been considered before her reign began in 1702. By the Act of Settlement 1701, if Anne left no issue of her own, the crown was to pass to her cousin, Sophia of Hanover, and then to Sophia's Protestant heirs. No Catholic can succeed to the throne of Great Britain.

Accordingly, while Anne's half-brother, James, had the strongest claim to the crown – stronger even than hers – he was denied it because he was a Catholic. And so were the better claims of 55 others. In the event Sophia died two months before Anne, and the crown passed instead to her son, George of Hanover, who became King George I of Great Britain and Ireland in 1714. George's native language was German and at the start of his reign he spoke to his British ministers in French. This made him unpopular with the British people.

Supporters of James' claim to the throne were known as Jacobites, and he was recognised as the King by Catholic France and Spain. Support was particularly strong in Scotland, and James made unsuccessful attempts to win the crown, with French assistance. Jacobite revolts in Scotland and England were to continue for half a century.

1721

The first Member of Parliament
said to have the Prime Minister role

Is a First Lord of the Treasury called
Robert Walpole

1721: ROBERT WALPOLE – FIRST PRIME MINSTER

Following the Glorious Revolution in 1688-89, the balance of power between the Crown and Parliament shifted decisively to Parliament. While Acts of Parliament required the consent of the Monarch, no consent was ever refused after 1708. While the Sovereign formally governed, they did so through their Ministers, and those Ministers had to get the backing of Parliament. A party system began to evolve. At first the main division was between members who supported reform, known as Whigs, and the more conservative, known as Tories.

The most important Minister of the Crown was known as the First Lord of the Treasury, and when the Whig Member of Parliament, Robert Walpole, was appointed to this position, as well as Chancellor of the Exchequer and Leader of the House of Commons, in 1721, he began to be referred to as the Prime Minister. Although this did not become a formal title until the start of the 20th Century, Walpole is considered to be Britain's first Prime Minister. He is also the longest serving, because he occupied this position for nearly 21 years, until 1742.

Walpole was an outstanding and persuasive orator, and gained popularity with both the King and the electorate by pursuing moderate policies. He sought to improve prosperity by avoiding war and promoting trade, and was largely successful. He had enjoyed a rapid rise after first entering Parliament in 1701, but was expelled from Parliament and imprisoned in the Tower of London for 6 months after being found guilty of corruption in 1712. But he was quickly re-elected and rose to prominence again when George I became King in 1714. George favoured the Whigs over the Tories, who he feared had Jacobite sympathies. Walpole lost a vote of confidence in the Commons in 1742, and resigned, having failed to prevent a war with Spain over a trading dispute, known as the War of Jenkin's Ear.

1746

*At Culloden the Jacobites finally
lose the fight to be royal*

*In the last ever pitched battle on
British soil*

1746: BATTLE OF CULLODEN

George II, succeeded to the British throne in 1727 on the death of his father, George I. George II had arrived in Britain when his father became King in 1714, and had immediately become Prince of Wales. Like his father he was born in Hanover, in what is now Germany, becoming the last British monarch to be born outside of Britain. Also like his father, he spent a considerable portion of his reign in his dukedom in Hanover, where his ruling powers were not limited by Parliament, as they were in Britain. In 1743 he led an army consisting of British, Hanoverian and allied troops at the Battle of Dettingen during the War of Austrian Succession, the last time a reigning British monarch was to personally lead troops into battle.

In 1746 his forces, led by his youngest son, the Duke of Cumberland, defeated the last serious attempt by the deposed James II's son, James Stuart, and his Jacobite supporters, to recover the British crown for the House of Stuart. James Stuart was referred to as the Old Pretender, and in 1745 his son, Charles Stuart, who became known as the New Pretender or Bonnie Prince Charles, had landed in Scotland and quickly raised an army, principally from Highland clans, who remained loyal to the Jacobite cause. Charles rapidly defeated George II's army in Scotland and marched his forces into England. The Duke of Cumberland and British forces were recalled from Europe, and marched against the Jacobite army, forcing its retreat back into Scotland. The decisive battle occurred on Culloden Moor, near Inverness, on the 16 April 1746. It was the last pitched battle on British soil, and lasted less than an hour. Charles' army, armed with mostly French supplied muskets and limited cannons, were no match for the larger numbers and superior artillery of Cumberland's forces. The Jacobites were defeated, and many of those that escaped hunted down and killed. Charles evaded capture for 5 months before successfully fleeing to France. He was never to return.

1769

*To unleash the power of steam
James Watt found a solution*

*Creating not just a better pump, but
an industrial revolution*

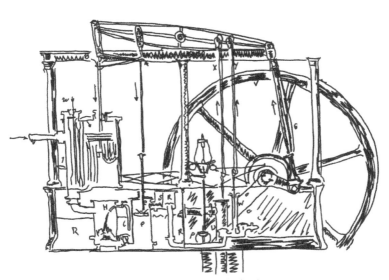

Machine à balancier de Watt

1769: JAMES WATT

James Watt, who was born in Scotland in 1736, did not invent the steam engine. The fact that steam, produced from heating water, could be used to power a pump had been known for some time before English inventor, Thomas Newcomen, created a steam powered water pump, known as the Newcomen engine, in 1712. James Watt realised that the Newcomen engine could be made a lot more efficient by adding a separate chamber, in which the steam could cool back to water before being recycled back to the boiler. This simple, but ground-breaking idea, was patented by Watt in 1769 – giving him the exclusive right to exploit it commercially. Watt continued to develop his invention, and produced a steam engine capable of turning a wheel, which meant it could do a lot more than just pump water. He had created the means to mechanise the manufacturing process for many items, setting in train the industrial revolution.

Watt went on to form a successful partnership with Matthew Boulton, a specialist in iron working, which was to last for 25 years. An extension was granted to Watt's patent by an Act of Parliament in 1775, giving the partnership a monopoly in the manufacture of steam engines based on his invention until 1800. When the patent ran out, Watt retired. While Watt was responsible for many other inventions and discoveries, including an early paper copying machine, none compared with the impact of his steam engine. He died in 1819.

Watt invented the term "horsepower" in order to describe the power of his engines. At the time horses were still used to turn mill wheels, and, in selling his engines, Watt could refer to the number of horses they would replace. The standard unit of measurement for power is today called a "watt", so named, in 1882, by the British Association for the Advancement of Science, in recognition of Watt's work.

1770

Australia claimed by endeavour of Captain Cook

Who sailed around the World and had a look

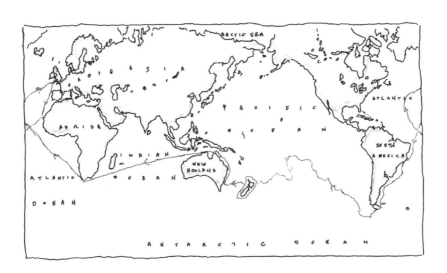

1770: JAMES COOK CLAIMS AUSTRALIA

England started to create permanent colonies in North America and the Caribbean from early in the reign of James I. These were often founded by trading companies, established to exploit the commercial opportunities such territories would create. The first American settlement of Jamestown, in 1607, was managed by the Virginia Company, which had been given a royal charter by James in 1606. Throughout the 1600s other companies were formed and English colonies spread across the Eastern side of North America, and the lucrative Caribbean islands. Tobacco and sugar were particularly profitable, and slaves were shipped from Africa to work on the plantations. In the 1700s the British East India Company, which had been chartered in 1600, spread its activities in Asia and came to rule large areas of India from 1757.

Australia had first been visited by Europeans in 1606, and was named "New Holland" by the Dutch in 1644. In 1768 the British Royal Navy Captain, James Cook, with his ship HMS Endeavour, was sent on an expedition to the Pacific Ocean. He sailed around New Zealand, and landed at Botany Bay in Australia in 1770. He named the eastern side of Australia New South Wales and claimed it for Britain. Australia was then progressively colonised by the British from 1783 onwards. Over the next 80 years more than 160,000 convicts were transported to a number of penal colonies established in Australia. The practice was ended in 1868.

James Cook was to make two more famous voyages. His second, from 1772 to 1775, saw him explore further the southern Pacific Ocean and return to New Zealand. His third voyage, from 1776, was intended to try and find a sea passage over the top of North America. On this trip he was killed by villagers on the island of Hawaii in 1779.

1776

Britain's empire will be the world's biggest we are told

But Washington's fight meant American colonies left the fold

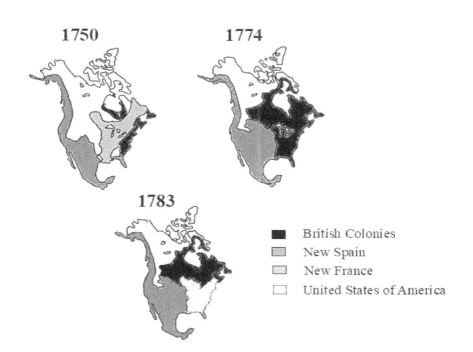

1750

1774

1783

British Colonies
New Spain
New France
United States of America

1776: AMERICAN WAR OF INDEPENDENCE

When George III succeeded his grandfather to the throne, in 1760, Britain was in the middle of the Seven Years War, the name given to a period from 1756 to 1763 when the great European powers fought one another for control of territory all over the world. In North America, Britain succeeded in extending its colonies northwards and westwards across what had been called New France. George Washington, who was later to lead the colonists' revolt against British rule, fought in the British Army against the French in this successful war.

After the war Britain was in great need of additional revenue to pay for accumulated debts and the greater costs of a bigger empire. However, when Parliament sought to impose taxes on the 13 American colonies, the colonists objected and revolted on the grounds that they were British subjects who had no representation in the British Parliament, and that therefore the British Parliament had no right to impose taxes on them. When the British government, led by the Prime Minister, Lord North, tried to assert its authority, the colonists established their own local parliaments, known as Congresses, and these sent representatives to a Continental Congress. This Congress declared a boycott of British goods and demanded freedom to determine their own internal affairs. Parliament would not agree, and war broke out in June 1775, the Congress having appointed Washington as their military leader. On the 4th July 1776 Congress made a declaration of independence from British rule. While the professional British Army initially enjoyed the most success, matters changed when the French and then the Spanish gave their support to the rebels. When the British surrendered to French and Washington forces at Yorktown on 19 October 1781 war was essentially over. The House of Commons voted to stop fighting in early 1782, and Lord North resigned. The war was formally ended by the Treaty of Paris, in 1783, when Britain recognised the new United States of America.

1796

Jenner's smallpox vaccine was really clever

World's biggest killer is now gone forever

1796: EDWARD JENNER – SMALLPOX VACCINE

King George III reigned for 60 years, from 1760 to 1820, but in his later years suffered from mental illness, and from 1811 to 1820 his son, George, ruled as Prince Regent, in a period known as the Regency. When his son succeeded him, and became King George IV, one of his first acts was to appoint an English doctor and scientist, called Edward Jenner, as a physician to the King.

Jenner was born in Berkley in Gloucestershire in 1749. After training as a surgeon in London from the age of 14, he returned to Berkley in 1773 and remained there as a family doctor. Jenner was interested in nature, and was one of the first to realise that birds, such as swallows, did not hibernate for the winter, but flew south. But his biggest discovery was one that completely transformed human life. He discovered the means of eradicating the smallpox virus. Smallpox had devastated peoples around the world for more than 1,000 years. By the end of the 18th Century, two thirds of Europe's population became infected with smallpox, a third of those dying from it and many of those that survived were left blind or horribly disfigured.

In 1796, after noticing that milkmaids who had had a much less virulent disease, called cowpox, rarely caught smallpox, Jenner carried out an experiment with his gardener's 8 year old son in which he first inserted the discharge from cowpox pustules into a cut in the boys arm and six weeks later injected him with pus from a smallpox sufferer. The boy did not develop smallpox, and Jenner then successfully repeated the experiment with 20 others. Jenner called the procedure vaccine inoculation or vaccination for short. Vaccination became accepted, and was eventually to be applied globally, eradicating smallpox entirely in 1978, following an intensive campaign. Smallpox had killed an estimated 300 million people in the 20th Century alone.

1800

Anglican politicians in Britain and Ireland worry that they will get too much sway

But Irish Catholics also agree union of the nations is the only way

AN

A C T

FOR

The Union of Great Britain and Ireland.

DUBLIN

1800

1800: ACTS OF UNION – GREAT BRITAIN AND IRELAND

In 1155 Pope Adrian IV had asked the English King, Henry II, to take control of Ireland. From Roman times the papacy itself claimed sovereignty over Ireland. For this reason, after Henry II invaded Ireland in 1171, he made his son, John, Lord of Ireland rather than King in 1177, and all English monarchs from King John onwards were styled Lord of Ireland. However, after Henry VIII's split from the Pope and the Catholic Church, he was made King of Ireland by the Crown of Ireland Act passed by the Irish Parliament in 1542. Thereafter England and Ireland, and after 1603 also Scotland, were each separate kingdoms of the same monarch. When England and Scotland united as the single kingdom of Great Britain in 1707, the Irish Parliament expressed the hope that Ireland might be able to join the same union. While Ireland remained politically separated, it was largely subservient to Great Britain.

Although the majority of Ireland's population was Catholic, most of the land, and all of the power, rested with members of the Church of Ireland, the Irish equivalent of the Protestant Church of England – churches in both being referred to as Anglican churches. As in England, Irish Catholics looked to end restrictions and achieve the same powers and freedoms enjoyed by Protestants, a process known as Catholic Emancipation. In 1798, there was a major rebellion by Irish Catholics, encouraged by the 1789 French Revolution and its ideals of freedom and equality, and actually supported by a French Army, which had landed in Ireland. It was suppressed by British forces in a bloody fashion. The British were concerned that the Catholic majority in Ireland would eventually hold sway, and therefore pushed for a union with Great Britain. The Irish Catholics were also promised emancipation by the English Prime Minister, William Pitt the Younger, and came to favour union, and the Irish Parliament eventually agreed. Acts of Union were passed in both Parliaments in 1800, and they became one in 1801.

19th CENTURY

In the 19th Century Victorian industry makes Britain the greatest imperial nation

While social and political reforms at home bring people participation

19th CENTURY (1801 to 1900)

Monarchs of Great Britain and Ireland

George III	1760-1820	Hanover
George IV	1820-1830	Hanover
William IV	1830-1837	Hanover
Victoria	1837-1901	Hanover

Prime Ministers of Great Britain and Ireland

William Pitt the Younger	1801	Tory
Henry Addington	1801-1804	Tory
William Pitt the Younger	1804-1806	Tory
Baron Grenville	1806-1807	Whig
Duke of Portland	1807-1809	Tory
Spencer Perceval	1809-1812	Tory
Earl of Liverpool	1812-1827	Tory
George Canning	1827	Tory
Viscount Goderich	1827-1828	Tory
Duke of Wellington	1828-1830	Tory
Earl Grey	1830-1834	Whig
Viscount Melbourne	1834	Whig
Duke of Wellington	1834	Tory
Sir Robert Peel	1834-1835	Conservative
Viscount Melbourne	1835-1841	Whig
Sir Robert Peel	1841-1846	Conservative
Lord John Russell	1846-1852	Whig
Earl of Derby	1852	Conservative
Earl of Aberdeen	1852-1855	Conservative
Viscount Palmerston	1855-1858	Whig
Earl of Derby	1858-1859	Conservative
Viscount Palmerston	1859-1865	Liberal
Earl Russell	1865-1866	Liberal
Earl of Derby	1866-1868	Conservative
Benjamin Disraeli	1868	Conservative
William Gladstone	1868-1874	Liberal
Benjamin Disraeli	1874-1880	Conservative
William Gladstone	1880-1885	Liberal
Marquess of Salisbury	1885-1886	Conservative
William Gladstone	1886	Liberal
Marquess of Salisbury	1886-1892	Conservative
William Gladstone	1892-1894	Liberal
Earl of Rosebery	1894-1895	Liberal
Marquess of Salisbury	1895-1902	Conservative

1804

Trevithick invented the steam locomotive, but who remembers his name?

Robert Stephenson's Rocket arrived down the line and grabbed all the fame

1804: FIRST STEAM LOCOMOTIVE

Richard Trevithick was a mine engineer born in Cornwall in 1771. From an early age he was fascinated by the steam engines used to pump water from Cornish Copper and Tin mines, and in 1797 he married the daughter of the owner of a company that made such engines. Working as an engineer at a mine in that year, Trevithick created a high-pressure steam engine. Rather than relying on air pressure to push a piston back and James Watts' condensing chamber, Trevithick's engine used two pistons working together driven by high pressure steam, which was exhausted out of a vertical chimney. The design allowed for a more powerful and smaller steam engine, which Trevithick was able mount on wheels and use to propel those wheels, creating a road locomotive in 1801, which he called "Puffing Devil".

Trevithick's first track locomotive resulted from a bet on whether his steam locomotive could pull 10 tons of iron ore for nearly 10 miles on the Merthyr Tydfil tramroad, which he won in February 1804. It took 4 hours at an average speed of only 2.5 miles an hour. While Trevithick was unable to create a locomotive that was really superior to horses at pulling wagons, others were soon to do so.

In 1829 a competition was organised by the Liverpool and Manchester Railway to find a steam locomotive to pull the first passenger train. The trial was won by Robert Stephenson's Rocket, which could reach speeds of 30 miles per hour. After a mishap at the opening ceremony for the first passenger train line in 1830, when the Member of Parliament for Liverpool, William Huskisson, was run over and killed by Rocket, Robert Stephenson's company led the way in building steam locomotives for railways in the western world for many years. Steam locomotives, which had to carry water and fuel, usually coal, along with them, were eventually replaced with diesel and electric trains in the 20th Century.

1805

A naval battle off the Cape of Trafalgar with a smaller British fleet

Is famous for Nelson's victory and a French and Spanish defeat

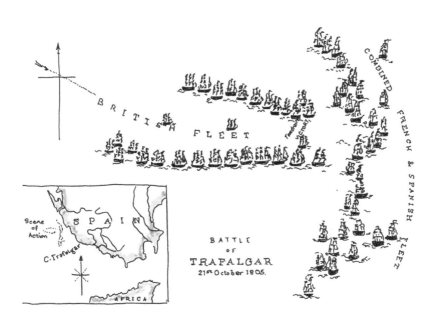

1805: BATTLE OF TRAFALGAR

The Parliamentary system of government, under a constitutional monarchy, was well established in Britain by the end of the 18th Century. In France however, the removal of their absolute monarch, Louis XVI, in a bloody Revolution starting in 1789, led first to a period known as the Reign of Terror, and then to the emergence of a brilliant soldier, Napoleon Bonaparte, who gained popular support, seized control of the government and in 1804 made himself Emperor of the French. He also established French military dominance over continental Europe through a series of successful wars. His ambition to invade Britain was, however, thwarted by the control the British Royal Navy exercised over the seas, and in particular the English Channel, where they blockaded Napoleon's ports.

In 1805 Napoleon planned to break the blockades using the French fleet in the Mediterranean together with the fleet of his then ally, Spain. The British Admiral, Lord Nelson, from his flagship, HMS Victory, commanded a fleet of 27 ships of the line against a superior French and Spanish fleet of 33 ships. The decisive sea battle took place on 21 October 1805 off the Cape of Trafalgar in southwestern Spain. As the battle was about to commence, Nelson famously sent a signal to all of his ships: "England expects that every man will do his duty". Nelson adopted an unusual battle formation, dividing his fleet into two columns, and sailing them rapidly towards and through the enemy line of ships. His plan worked and the successful British fleet won the battle without losing a single ship. His enemy lost 22 ships. Nelson lived just long enough to learn that the battle was won. He was fatally wounded by a musket bullet from a French marksman as HMS Victory cut through the enemy. Victory itself was saved at one stage by another British ship, HMS Temeraire. This celebrated sea battle ended Napoleon's hope of conquering Britain, and made Lord Nelson a national hero.

1807

Across the British Empire thanks to William Wilberforce

No human slave can be traded in the same way as a horse

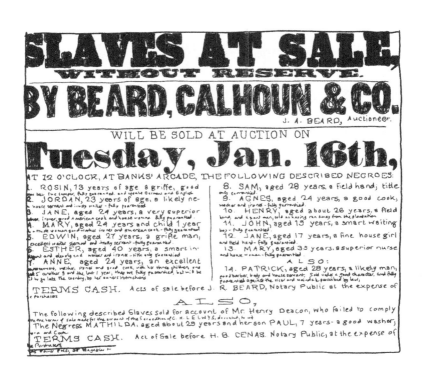

1807: ABOLITION OF THE SLAVE TRADE

As the European powers colonised the Americas, principally Spain and Portugal in South and Central America, and England and France in North America and the Caribbean, they looked for large quantities of cheap labour to work in Gold and Silver mines and on plantations growing sugar, cotton, tobacco and other valuable commodities. From the start of the 1500s they supplied that need for labour by buying slaves from African leaders and shipping them across the Atlantic. Over the next 400 years it is estimated that more than 11 million Africans were so shipped as slaves, with more than 10 percent dying on the sea voyage itself due to the poor cramped conditions aboard ship.

By the late 1700s British ships were responsible for much of the slave trade, supplying the colonies of all of the European powers with many of their African slaves. In 1783 a British Protestant group, known as the Quakers, presented Parliament with the first anti-slave trade petition, and the campaign was taken up by an evangelical Christian, and Yorkshire Member for Parliament, William Wilberforce. From early on his campaign had the support of the Prime Minister, William Pitt the Younger, who was a close friend of Wilberforce, and by many Christian groups. While the campaign appeared to enjoy popular support, this waned considerably as a conservative reaction to the French Revolution in 1789, and the first Parliamentary bill to abolish the slave trade, introduced by Wilberforce in 1791, was voted down by a significant majority. Wilberforce continued his campaign and in 1804 he persuaded the House of Commons to support his bill, but it then ran out of time. In 1806 Pitt died, but the new Prime Minister, Lord Grenville supported the cause. The Foreign Slave Act was passed in May 1806, banning British subjects from selling slaves to French colonies, and in 1807 The Slave Trade Act prohibited all slave trading across the Empire. Slavery was later abolished by the Slavery Abolition Act 1833.

1815

Emperor Napoleon's attempt to retake Europe ends at Waterloo

When Wellington gives him the boot and the Prussians do too

1815: WATERLOO

In the first decade of the 19th Century, Napoleon Bonaparte established a French Empire consisting of most of Western Europe. The territory he controlled included Spain, Italy and much of what is now Germany, together with extensive colonies in the Americas, Africa and south east Asia. He was engaged in almost constant warfare. As the British blockaded French ports, to prevent a French invasion, Napoleon responded with what became known as the Continental system – prohibiting European countries from trading with Britain. In the midst of joining in various coalitions fighting against Napoleon, Britain went to war again with the United States, in 1812, successfully defending British colonies in Canada. But the main focus was fighting in what became known as the Napoleonic wars.

In 1808 Napoleon occupied Spain, his former ally, and installed his brother Joseph as its King. This set off the Peninsular War, in which the British Army, led by the Duke of Wellington, fought alongside Spaniards seeking to restore the Bourbon monarchy. This war lasted 6 years, ending in Napoleon's defeat in 1814, after Napoleon had depleted his strength in 1812, when he attempted to invade Russia with a huge French Army and after reaching Moscow was then forced to retreat losing most of his men in the Russian winter. In April 1814, the allied nations having captured Paris, forced Napoleon to abdicate. Louis XVIII became King of France, with the monarchy restored. However, very shortly Napoleon escaped from exile on the island of Elba, returned to France, regained control of the French Army and restored himself as Emperor. He was finally defeated at the famous battle of Waterloo on 18 June 1815, by the British Army led by Wellington and Prussian forces. Napoleon was exiled to the remote island of Saint Helena, where he died in 1821. Napoleon's defeat was followed by the Congress of Vienna, which significantly reshaped Europe.

1831

For the invention of electric motors and power generators it is Faraday we owe

For he discovered that moving magnets around a wire induces electricity to flow

Michael Faraday

1831: FARADAY – ELECTROMAGNETIC INDUCTION

Michael Faraday was born in South London in 1791. His family was not wealthy, and he lacked a formal education, but from the age of 14 he worked as an apprentice to a bookseller, and he was able to educate himself by reading many books. He developed an interest in science and in 1812 attended some lectures given by Humphry Davey at the Royal Institution. Davey was a notable chemist, who was later to invent the Davy Lamp for use in coalmines. This lamp enclosed its flame with a fine gauze which allowed the lamp to burn but prevented it from igniting flammable gases which often escaped into mine shafts, thus saving many miners' lives. Davy was so impressed with Faraday's notes of his lectures that he appointed him as Chemical Assistant at the Royal Institution in 1813.

Faraday was a brilliant experimentalist, and was responsible for many significant discoveries and inventions. He was particularly interested in investigating the properties of electricity and magnetism. He discovered the laws of electrolysis, a process where electricity is used to cause chemical reactions and separate elements. At that time there existed rudimentary electrical batteries, and it was noticed that electricity flowing through a wire created a magnetic field around the wire. Faraday successfully reversed this effect in 1831. By passing a magnet through a loop of wire he was able to create a flow of electricity along the wire. Not only had he proven the fundamental relationship between electricity and magnetism, which we call electromagnetism, but he had discovered the principle of electromagnetic induction, which would lead to the development of electrical motors and power generators. Faraday himself created the first electric dynamo, in which a copper disk was turned by hand through a horseshoe magnet to generate an electric current. A devout and modest Christian, Faraday turned down a knighthood in 1832. He died in 1867.

1832

A chaotic and rotten electoral system is bound to fail

Great Reform gives vote to one in five of those who are adult, and male

1832: THE GREAT REFORM ACT

By the time William IV became King of Great Britain and Ireland, on the death of his brother George IV, in 1830, the supremacy of Parliament was well established. In general, the government was led by a Prime Minister whose political party, Whig or Tory, could command a majority in the House of Commons - although the Prime Minister himself was often a member of the House of Lords. While elections for the House of Commons were regularly held, the electoral system itself was archaic and corrupt. There were two types of constituencies – counties and boroughs, which generally returned 2 members each. While the qualification to vote usually depended on land ownership, the requirements varied greatly from place to place. Moreover, because the boroughs had often been chosen centuries earlier, with population movement, the size of the electorate choosing its 2 members varied dramatically. The largest, Westminster, had 12,000 voters, while a few, known as rotten boroughs, had only a handful. Corruption was rife, and the majority of the seats were effectively in the gift of a powerful patron and were frequently bought and sold.

Towns and cities which had grown massively in the industrial revolution were particularly unrepresented. Birmingham and Manchester did not enjoy representation, and became centres for large electoral reform rallies. Eleven protestors were killed when a huge such rally was suppressed at St. Peter Fields in Manchester in 1819, an event which came to be called the Peterloo massacre. Eventually the demand for reform won the day and Whig Prime Minister, Earl Grey, was able to pass the Representation of the People Act, known as the Great Reform Act, in 1832, and separate Acts covering Scotland and Ireland, which extended the franchise and abolished the worst abuses. While still only one in five adult males were eligible to vote, it marked the start of the reforms which were to eventually lead to a universal right to vote.

1837

From the 18 year old daughter of the 4th son of King George the Third

Comes the Victorian age of invention and power and a people who are reserved

1837: QUEEN VICTORIA

The names of the two main political groupings in Parliament at the start of the 19th Century, "Whig" and "Tory", were originally terms of abuse given by one political faction to the other in the 17th Century. Whigs tended to favour a constitutional monarchy and reform, while Tories tended to resist change. Between 1721 and 1783 Whigs were in power for all but 3 years, but as a result of voter repulsion with the French Revolution in 1789, and the Napoleonic wars that followed, the position reversed and from 1783 to 1830 the Tories were in control for all but 1 year. There then followed 4 years of Whig reformist government from 1830 to 1834, under Earl Grey, who passed the Great Reform Act and finally abolished slavery throughout the British Empire, and then, briefly, under Viscount Melbourne. The Tories came back in 1834, under Sir Robert Peel, who transformed the Tories into the Conservative Party.

When Queen Victoria came to the throne in 1837, on the death of her uncle William IV, she had just turned 18, and Melbourne was once again the Whig Prime Minister. Victoria's father, Edward, Duke of Kent, who had died when she was 1, was the fourth son of George III, but none of his elder brothers had been survived by legitimate children. While Victoria became Queen of the United Kingdom, she did not succeed William IV to the crown of Hanover, as Hanover law did not allow for a female monarch, and instead her father's younger brother, Ernest Augustus, became King of Hanover.

Victoria married Prince Albert of Saxe-Coburg and Gotha in 1840. She was to reign for nearly 64 years, and gave her name to a period in which huge advances occurred in all areas of life and the British Empire grew to become the biggest empire the World had ever seen. Victoria, who was known for strict moral values and reserve, had 9 children, who were to marry into Royal families across Europe.

1838

JMW Turner, an artist beyond compare

Painted Britain's greatest painting, The Fighting Temeraire

1838: JMW TURNER – THE FIGHTING TEMERAIRE

Britain's two most celebrated artists, JMW Turner and John Constable, were born just over a year apart, in the reign of George III, in 1775 and 1776. Turner came from very humble beginnings. He was the son of a barber and was born in Covent Garden in London. Constable, on the other hand, was the son of a wealthy corn merchant and born in Suffolk. While they both became renowned as landscape painters, their styles were very different. Turner, who was to enjoy the far greater success during his lifetime, developed an atmospheric style intended to convey what the art critic, John Ruskin, called the "moods of nature" through light and colour, while Constable painted beautiful rural scenes, such as his best known oil painting "The Hay Wain", which was first exhibited at the Royal Academy's exhibition in 1821.

Turner's artistic talent had been recognised very young, and he had been accepted into the Royal Academy at the age of 15, in 1790. He was to leave more than 500 oil paintings and 2,000 watercolours, and was to inspire many later painters, including the French impressionist Claude Monet. Turner's most popular work was a seascape called "The Fighting Temeraire", which he painted in 1838. This depicted the HMS Temeraire, which had played a crucial part in rescuing Lord Nelson's flagship at the Battle of Trafalgar, 33 years earlier, being towed by a steam tug along the River Thames to a breaker's yard at Rotherhithe, while the sun sets. Turner personally witnessed the event, and his beautiful painting symbolised the transition from sail ships to ships driven by steam engines in the industrial revolution.

Before his death in 1837, Constable gave popular public lectures on the history of landscape painting. While Turner, despite being the most highly regarded artist of his time, became more reclusive and eccentric. He died of cholera in 1851 and was buried in St Paul's Cathedral.

1839

Dickens is popular for showing the true lives of the poor

And Oliver Twist has them asking for more

1839: CHARLES DICKENS – OLIVER TWIST

Born in Portsmouth in 1812, and having been forced to work in a shoe blacking factory at the age of 12, when his father was sent to a debtor's prison, Charles Dickens was to become the greatest Victorian writer. Before he started his literary career, in 1833, he had worked as a solicitor's clerk and as a parliamentary reporter and journalist. He had seen and experienced first-hand the lives of the poorest in society, and the legal and political systems for managing society, of which he was highly critical. In 1849, in a letter he wrote to the Times newspaper, to express his horror at witnessing a public execution attended by 30,000 spectators, Dickens wrote: "I have seen, habitually, some of the worst sources of general contamination and corruption in this country, and I think there are not many phases of London life that could surprise me".

Oliver Twist; or, the Parish Boy's Progress was originally published as a serial in a magazine between 1837 and 1839. It was Dickens' second novel, after *The Pickwick Papers,* and tells the story of a young orphan who grew up in a workhouse and had the audacity to ask for more food. He eventually escaped to London and experienced life in the criminal underworld before eventually being saved. The novel cast light on the extraordinary harshness of the workhouse system then in operation. At that time, and since the Relief of the Poor Act 1601, local parishes were responsible for caring for those who could not work, and the poor were supported by a local property tax. Workhouses grew up in the 17th Century as a way of reducing the need for poor relief, by providing accommodation and food to the poor in return for work.

Other Dickens novels were to contain biting social commentary, albeit with colourful and often humorous characters, including *Hard Times*, *Nicholas Nickleby, Bleak House, David Copperfield* and *A Christmas Carol.* Dickens died, and was buried in Westminster Abbey, in 1870.

1840

The Penny Black stamp and the advent of rail

Now post is pre-paid and arrives without fail

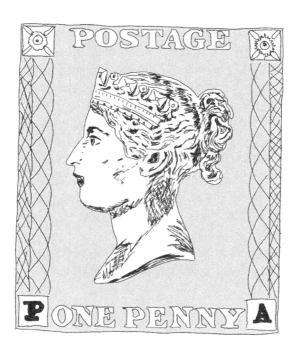

1840: FIRST POSTAGE STAMP

The first public postal system was introduced by Charles I in 1635, when he made the Royal Mail, created by Henry VIII in 1516, available to everyone. Before that time people had to arrange their own messengers to carry letters, but now they could use Royal Mail staff, and its network of post roads and offices – which expanded to towns across the country. Until 1840 it was usual for the recipient to pay for any letters they received, although there was a variety of practices and rates depending on weight and distance.

A uniform postage rate was proposed by the social reformer, Rowland Hill, in 1837, and he was given responsibility for creating a new postal system. In January 1840 he introduced the Uniform Penny Post – which made a fixed charge of one penny for pre-paid letters, or two pennies if the money was collected from the recipient. To facilitate this system, he introduced a sticker to put on letters, the first of which was called the Penny Black – which was the world's first postage stamp. This stamp lasted only a year, because it was realised that black was not a good colour for a stamp as it made cancellation marks difficult to make out, and it was replaced with the Penny Red. The Penny Black, and all stamps afterwards, contained an image of the monarch. Throughout Queen Victoria's 64 year reign the same image of her was used, first drawn in 1837. Unlike the stamps of all other countries of the world, British stamps do not contain the name of the country.

The rapid growth of the British railway network, from 98 miles of track in 1830 to 10,433 miles of track in 1860, coupled with the fast improvements in steam locomotives, was fully exploited by Royal Mail to allow letters to be delivered quicker and more cheaply. The first trains with Travelling Post Offices on them, allowing mail to be sorted on the move, were introduced as early as 1838.

1841

Railways, tunnels, bridges and ships are all here

Because Isambard Kingdom Brunel was a great engineer

SS Great Britain

1841: GREAT WESTERN RAILWAY – BRUNEL

Isambard Kingdom Brunel was born in Portsmouth in 1806, the son of the eminent engineer, Marc Brunel. His father was born in France, but had fled to America following the French Revolution and had been the Chief Engineer of New York city before coming to England in 1799, where he undertook projects for the British government. His skills as an engineer were so valued by the government, that when he found himself in the debtors' prison in 1821, the government agreed to pay his debts. He sent his son to France, at the age of 14, to be educated in engineering, and on his return to England, Brunel worked with his father on a project to create a tunnel under the River Thames, and narrowly escaped death when it flooded in 1828.

In 1831 Brunel won a competition to design the Clifton Suspension Bridge over the River Avon in Bristol. This was one of many bridges that Brunel was to design. In 1833 he was made the chief engineer for the Great Western Railway, and tasked with constructing a railway line from London to Bristol. In fact Brunel's ambition went well beyond this, as he envisaged a journey from London to New York, the first part by a train from London to the west of Wales and then a second part on a steamship across the Atlantic to New York. Not only did Brunel design the Great Western rail line to Bristol, which opened in 1841, complete with bridges and tunnels, including the nearly 2 mile long Box Tunnel near Bath, but he also designed the *SS Great Western* steamship. He followed this with the first iron hulled steamship using a screw propeller rather than a paddle-wheel, the *SS Great Britain*, launched in 1843. At nearly 100 metres long this was the world's largest ship.

Brunel was involved in many other projects, which while not always successful, were noted for their innovative ideas. He is considered Britain's greatest engineer. He died in 1859, at the age of 53.

1851

Prince Albert organises Great Exhibition in Hyde Park for all to see That industry and technology can set man free

1851: THE GREAT EXHIBITION

When Queen Victoria married Prince Albert of Saxe-Coburg and Gotha in the third year of her reign, in 1840, she found not only the love of her life, but a conscientious supporter, who took up a number of public causes. Albert not only ran the Royal Household, but promoted reforms in education and worked to eradicate slavery in the rest of the world beyond the British Empire. Albert was also particularly interested in science and innovation, and the application of these in industry to create better conditions for all.

Albert was one of the principal organisers of the Great Exhibition of the Works of Industry of All Nations, which took place in Hyde Park in London in the Summer of 1851. The Great Exhibition was a notable success, with 13,000 exhibits from all over the World, but showcasing the products of British engineering and the industrial revolution. The exhibition was put together in just 9 months, and this included the design and construction of a huge glass and iron framed building to house it, which was called the Crystal Palace. This building, which Isambard Kingdom Brunel helped to design, was 565 metres long, 138 metres wide and 39 metres high.

Six million people visited the exhibition, which was a third of the population of Britain, and the profits made from it were such that they were used to found the Science Museum, the Natural History Museum and the Victoria and Albert Museum, in nearby Kensington, in the following years.

Prince Albert, who was given the title Prince Consort by Victoria in 1857, died of typhoid fever, aged 42, in 1861. Victoria was devastated by his death, and wore black for the last 40 years of her reign. The Royal Albert Hall, opened in 1871, was named in Albert's memory.

1855

Florence, with her lamp, was the first who saw

Poor hygiene was the biggest killer of the Crimean War

1855: FLORENCE NIGHTINGALE

The Crimean War was fought from 1853 to 1856, when the United Kingdom allied with France to support the Ottoman Empire against encroachment from the Russian Empire in south east Europe. Having succeeded in their initial aim of repulsing Russian forces, the allies attacked Russia's naval base at Sevastopol in the Crimea, and defeated the Russians at the Battles of Alma and Balaclava in 1854. The Battle of Balaclava included the infamous charge of the light brigade, an ill-judged cavalry charge by the British directly into the face of Russian artillery. The war ended when Russia sued for peace in 1856.

Born in Florence in 1820, the daughter of a wealthy Englishman, who gave her an education well in advance of that usually given to girls at that time, Florence Nightingale became a household name as "the lady of lamp" during the Crimean War. Florence believed that she had a calling from god to care for the sick, and after receiving some medical training was pursuing her career in Harley Street when she persuaded her friend Sidney Herbert, the Secretary at War, to send her, with 38 volunteer nurses, to the Crimea to care for sick and wounded soldiers. Florence found conditions there appallingly unhygienic, with many more of the wounded dying from disease than their battle wounds. She demanded a solution from the British Government, which led to Isambard Kingdom Brunel being commissioned to create a pre-fabricated hospital, which was shipped to Turkey. This, and other sanitation measures, helped to dramatically reduce the death rate.

On her return to England, Florence created the Nightingale Fund for the training of nurses, and in 1859 she wrote *Notes on Nursing* which became the standard text for nurse training. She was a brilliant statistician and prolific writer, who although mostly bedridden for the last 53 years of her life, worked tirelessly to improve conditions for all.

1859

To add the theory of evolution to your book collection

Darwin's Origin of Species is a natural selection

It is the circumstance, that several of the islands possess their own species of the tortoise... that strikes me with wonder.

The Galapagos Tortoise

1859: CHARLES DARWIN – THE ORIGIN OF SPECIES

In the 1850s the majority of students graduating from Oxford and Cambridge Universities became Church of England clergymen, and when Charles Darwin's father enrolled him at Christ's College, Cambridge University in 1828, it was with a view to him becoming an Anglican country parson. Darwin was the son of a wealthy doctor, born in Shrewsbury in 1809. He had earlier attempted to study medicine at the University of Edinburgh from 1825, but was far more interested in studying the natural world and natural history. Darwin's own grandfather, Erasmus, had postulated a theory of evolution as early as 1794, but the prevailing wisdom was that life forms had been created by God and did not change. Indeed, it was still thought by many, based on the Bible story of creation, that the world itself was less than 6,000 years old. More than any other person, Darwin's meticulous studies and publications, were to convince other scientists, and the population in general, of evolution and the principle of natural selection. As Darwin wrote concerning life organisms: "favourable variations would tend to be preserved and unfavourable ones to be destroyed. The result would be the formation of a new species".

Darwin was able to develop his theories on a 5-year voyage around the world on HMS Beagle, working as a naturalist and geologist, from 1831. He observed the variations that existed in the same species in different places, and noted how their different characteristics assisted their survival in those places. In the Galapagos Islands, in the Pacific Ocean, he found small changes in the shape of tortoise shells on different islands. In 1859 he published a book setting out his theories, called *On the Origin of Species by Means of Natural Selection, or the Preservation of Favoured Races in the Struggle for Life.* It was an instant success, and was followed in 1871 by his book *The Descent of Man.* Darwin died in 1882, and was buried in Westminster Abbey, next to Sir Isaac Newton.

1865

When moving electrons meet a magnetic field energy waves take flight

We know that colours are simply different sizes of wave, because Maxwell saw the light

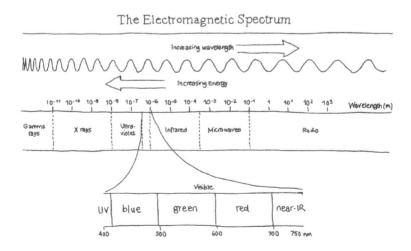

1865: JAMES CLERK MAXWELL – ELECTROMAGNETIC RADIATION

James Clerk Maxwell, born in Edinburgh in 1831, was a child genius and a brilliant student who after attending both Edinburgh and Cambridge Universities, became a professor of natural philosophy at Aberdeen at the age of just 25. While Maxwell made many contributions to scientific progress in a number of areas, including determining that the rings around the planet Saturn, which could be seen through telescopes, were not solid, but consisted of many small particles, he is best known for his work on electromagnetic radiation.

Michael Faraday, who was 40 years older than Maxwell, and with whom Maxwell became acquainted at the Royal Institution in his later years, had discovered the close interrelationship of electrical and magnetic fields, and how magnetism could induce electricity and vice versa. Maxwell took this work further. He studied the energy radiated outwards when electrical and magnetic fields interacted. Having calculated that this energy travelled at the speed of light, which had recently been discovered to be about 300 million metres a second, Maxwell concluded that light itself was a form of electromagnetic radiation, and that electricity, magnetism and light were all manifestations of the same substance. Electromagnetic waves were emitted at different frequencies depending on the vibration of the electric and magnetic fields which caused them, and it was later shown that radio waves, microwaves, x-rays, gamma rays and visible light are all simply electromagnetic waves of different frequencies. Light and colours were simply a band of electromagnetic wave frequencies that could be perceived through human eyes. Maxwell was also fascinated by colour vision, and the fact that all colours could be created with the 3 primary colours. He used his discoveries in this area to create the first colour photographs in 1861. Maxwell died of cancer in 1879. He is considered to be the greatest physicist of the 19th Century.

1870

If people are ignorant, they may be easier to rule

But now all children from 5 to 12 must go to school

1870: EDUCATION ACTS

When Lord Palmerston became Prime Minister for the second time, in 1859, his government was considered the first Liberal Government - the Liberals having emerged largely from the Whigs, and were supporters of reform and free trade. The Liberal Party was not formally so-called until 1868, in which year its leader, William Gladstone, won a large majority in the House of Commons in the first General Election after the Second Reform Act of 1867 had doubled the number of men eligible to vote. Gladstone was to serve as Prime Minister four times in the next 24 years, and championed the idea of equality of opportunity.

One of Gladstone's most significant achievements was to secure school education for all children under the age of 13. Children had always been a source of cheap labour, and indeed that was the main reason why many industrialists opposed Gladstone's reforms. There had been earlier efforts to support child education, such as the Factory Act 1833, which prohibited children under 9 working in factories, and provided that children from 9 to 13 could only be employed if they had 2 hours of schooling a day. At the time the Elementary Education Act 1870 was passed only half of children of primary school age attended school. The Act established elected school boards tasked with ensuring children from ages 5 to 12 had the opportunity to receive a school education in England and Wales. A similar Act for Scotland was passed in 1872. Such education still generally had to be paid for. The Elementary Education Act 1880, passed shortly after the start of Gladstone's second time as Prime Minister, made it illegal to employ a child under 13 who had not reached a minimum education standard. While there had been opposition to universal education from those who feared that educated masses would revolt, it was ultimately recognised that extending the right to vote made education essential, and that teaching all reading, writing and arithmetic was vital for the advancement of industry.

1875

Telecommunications are all fine and well

But for the first call, give us a bell.

1875: INVENTION OF THE TELEPHONE

The use of electricity to send communications in Britain began in 1837, when William Cooke and Charles Wheatstone, with some assistance from Michael Faraday, created an electrical telegraph system for use in conjunction with the English railway lines being constructed. The system allowed messages to be transmitted through pulses of electricity being sent down metal wires. The American, Samuel Morse, created a telegraph system that could record messages on paper tape with dots and dashes in the same year, and invented Morse Code, which became the international standard. When the insulation of wires was sufficiently improved, telegraph wire networks spread rapidly, particularly in the United States and the United Kingdom. In 1866 the Brunel designed, *SS Great Eastern*, was used to lay the first durable transatlantic telegraph cable between the two countries.

Alexander Graham Bell, a Scottish inventor born in 1847, took the idea further by inventing the telephone, which he patented while working in America in 1876. Bell had come from a family who specialised in work to improve speech, and he became an expert in this area – working in particular with deaf people, which included both his mother and his wife, to help them to communicate. In 1872 he had become the professor of Vocal Physiology and Elocution at Boston University. He conducted many experiments to artificially create the sounds of the human voice, and, from working with tuning forks, had realised the possibility of converting sound waves into changing electrical currents and then those back again into sound waves. With an experienced electrical engineer, Thomas Watson, he created an acoustic telegraph in 1875, which could transmit voice like sounds. The first real telephone call took place in 1876 when Bell told Watson over a short line that he wished to see him. The telephone revolutionised communication, and made Bell very rich. Bell died in Canada in 1922.

1876

When Disraeli decided her reign needed more euphoria

He handed the title of Empress of India to Queen Victoria

1876: EMPRESS OF INDIA

Benjamin Disraeli, who was born in Bloomsbury in 1804, was the most famous Victorian politician after William Gladstone, and served as a Conservative Prime Minister, briefly in 1868, and then from 1874 to 1880. In 1876, at the request of Queen Victoria, Disraeli pushed the Royal Titles Act 1876 through Parliament, which gave Victoria the title of Empress of India. A few months later Victoria elevated her Prime Minister to the House of Lords, making him the Earl of Beaconsfield.

Like a number of other British colonies, the conquest of India was achieved by a British trading company. In the case of India this was the East India Company, which was created by a royal charter from Queen Elizabeth I granted in 1600, and which was allowed to set up trading posts in India by the Mughal emperors from 1608. It slowly built up its influence and power, becoming a military as well as a trading enterprise. As the Mughal Empire collapsed the Company took control of the various princely states, fighting a number of battles to do so. By the 1800s the Company had a private army, most of whom were recruited locally, which was twice the size of the British army, and was in control of a large part of southern Asia. However, Indian resentment to the rule of the Company turned into a full-scale rebellion in 1857, which was known as the Indian Mutiny. While the rebellion was defeated, the East India Company was disbanded, and the British Government took direct control of India, with the Government of India Act 1858. The Act vested all of the Company's territories in Queen Victoria and allowed her to appoint a Governor-General for India, as well as Governors for the different regions. In practice the British Prime Minister and the Secretary of State for India exercised ultimate control. This period of British rule, which lasted until 1947, was known as the British Raj. Victoria's successors to the British throne were also known as Emperor of India until 1948.

1899

*Elgar's popular Enigma Variations
is only the first part of his story*

*As he marches on with pomp and
circumstance to the land of hope
and glory*

1899: EDWARD ELGAR

While Catholics remained barred from the Crown, the Catholic Relief Act 1829 had removed other restraints and disabilities, such as the right to sit in the House of Commons, hold military offices or work in the Civil Service. There nevertheless remained considerable prejudice against Catholics, and this was to affect the career of one of Britain's most popular classical music composers, Edward Elgar, who was a Catholic. When Elgar married the Anglican daughter of an army Major -General, in 1889, she was disinherited by her family.

Born near Worcester in 1857, Elgar came from a musical family. From 1872 he earned his living from teaching and performing music, and slowly he established a reputation as a composer, largely writing works for popular choir festivals. In 1899 he produced a piece of music which was hugely popular both in Britain and abroad, known as the *Enigma Variations*, and which included the extraordinarily beautiful *Nimrod*.

With the *Enigma Variations,* Elgar gained recognition as Britain's leading composer, and he went on to compose the *Pomp and Circumstances Marches*, including the music of *Land of Hope and Glory*, the words of which were provided by Arthur Benson for a concert celebrating the coronation of King Edward VII in 1902.

Elgar was knighted in 1904, and later in 1924 was appointed Master of the King's Music. Elgar embraced the invention of the gramophone, one of the first musicians to do so, and enthusiastically released recordings of his famous works.

Elgar died in 1934, in the same year as another great English composer, Gustav Holst, who had composed the ever popular, *The Planets* orchestral suite, between 1914 and 1916.

20th CENTURY

In the 20th Century liberal social democracies defeat authoritarian regimes

And a welfare state, technology and self-governance, allow peoples to follow their dreams

20th CENTURY (1901 to 2000)

Monarchs of Great Britain and Ireland/Northern Ireland (from 1949)

Victoria	1837-1901	Hanover
Edward VII	1901-1910	Saxe-Coburg and Gotha
George V	1910-1936	Windsor (from 1917)
Edward VIII	1936	Windsor
George VI	1936-1952	Windsor
Elizabeth II	1952-	Windsor

Prime Ministers of Great Britain and Ireland/Northern Ireland (from 1921)

Marquess of Salisbury	1895-1902	Conservative
Arthur Balfour	1902-1905	Conservative
Sir Henry Campbell-Bannerman	1905-1908	Liberal
H.H.Asquith	1908-1916	Liberal
David Lloyd George	1916-1922	Liberal
Bonar Law	1922-1923	Conservative
Stanley Baldwin	1923-1924	Conservative
Ramsay MacDonald	1924	Labour
Stanley Baldwin	1924-1929	Conservative
Ramsay McDonald	1929-1935	Labour (National from 1931)
Stanley Baldwin	1935-1937	Conservative
Neville Chamberlain	1937-1940	Conservative
Winston Churchill	1940-1945	Conservative
Clement Attlee	1945-1951	Labour
Winston Churchill	1951-1955	Conservative
Sir Anthony Eden	1955-1957	Conservative
Harold MacMillan	1957-1963	Conservative
Sir Alec Douglas-Home	1963-1964	Conservative
Harold Wilson	1964-1970	Labour
Edward Heath	1970-1974	Conservative
Harold Wilson	1974-1976	Labour
James Callaghan	1976-1979	Labour
Margaret Thatcher	1979-1990	Conservative
John Major	1990-1997	Conservative
Tony Blair	1997-2007	Labour

1901

The Queen dies and we are no longer Victorians

For the next decade of prosperity and social change we will be Edwardians

1901: EDWARD VII

When Queen Victoria died in January 1901, after more than 63 years on the throne, it not only brought to an end the longest reign of any British monarch up to that time, but her eldest son, who became King Edward VII, had also waited the longest time for the throne as the Prince of Wales. While Edward had been popular with the people, his flamboyant and pleasure-seeking life style scandalised his moral and reserved mother, who not only blamed his behaviour for the premature death of her husband, Prince Albert, in 1861, but she also tried to exclude him from all political involvement while she was the Queen.

Edward reigned until 1910, and although the period of his reign was barely 9 years, it was so distinctly different from what had preceded it, that it is known as the Edwardian era. Although the position of Britain as the world's leading power was now being rivalled by both the United States, and, more threateningly, the German Empire, there was considerable wealth in Britain and, as the saying went, the sun never sets on the British Empire, which then extended to large parts of all of the continents of the globe.

The Edwardian era was marked by considerable social and political change. The House of Lords was dominated by the large landowners, who tended to support the Conservative Party, while the government of the day was determined by the composition of the House of Commons. The convention had already been developed in the 19th Century that the Prime Minister should sit in the House of Commons, and the Conservative, Lord Salisbury, who left office in 1902, was the last Prime Minister to serve from the House of Lords. After the reform minded Liberals came to power again, under Henry Campbell-Bannerman, with a landslide victory in the 1906 General Election, the Lords' power to block social reforms would soon be severely curtailed.

1902

British scramble to take the right side of Africa from top to bottom in colonial wars

Hundreds of thousands are sent to recapture the South and defeat the Boers

1902: THE BOER WAR

Between 1884 and 1914 there was a period which became known as the Scramble for Africa, when the great European powers went from controlling relatively small areas around the edges to the almost complete colonisation of the entire continent. Britain and France were at the forefront of this, and by the end of that period Britain controlled some of the west and most of the east side of Africa, from Egypt at the top down to the Union of South Africa at the bottom.

The Boer War, which Britain was to win in 1902, after its biggest military engagement since the Napoleonic wars had ended in 1815, was fought to secure control of two of the richest regions of Southern Africa known as the Transvaal and the Orange Free State.

The Dutch had been the first to create a settlement in South Africa, in 1652. The Dutch territory was captured by the British in 1806, establishing the British Cape Colony. The Dutch word for farmer is "boer", and a large number of farmers, or Boers, sought to escape British rule by moving further into Africa, eventually establishing these two states. When diamonds and gold were discovered to exist, in vast quantities, in the region of the two states it attracted a large number of Europeans, particularly the British. When the British Government demanded that these Britons should enjoy voting rights in these states, the Boers declared war on Britain in 1899, and attacked the Cape Colony. After initial success, the Boars were overwhelmed by 400,000 British Empire troops that were sent to crush them. When the Boers resorted to guerrilla tactics, attacking strategic British positions, the British, led by Lord Kitchener, began a scorched earth policy, destroying large areas of Boer land and moving populations into concentration camps. This forced the Boers to surrender, and the two states became part of the Union of South Africa in 1910, within the British Empire.

1911

The Welfare State begins as the Liberals lay the first brick

A National Insurance scheme to help the poor when they are sick

1911: NATIONAL INSURANCE ACT

Following their victory in the 1906 General Election, the Liberal Party set about transforming British life with a series of welfare reforms. Under Prime Minister Henry Campbelll-Bannerman they passed legislation for free school meals and free education for secondary age children, and when HH Asquith replaced him, as the Liberal Prime Minister, in 1908, there began a serious effort to redistribute wealth to the poorest in society. This laid the foundations for the welfare state.

In 1909, Asquith's Chancellor of the Exchequer, David Lloyd George, proposed the People's Budget, which sought to raise income tax for higher earners, increase death duties and introduce a land tax, and which had the stated aim of eliminating poverty. The Finance Bill was passed by the House of Commons, but rejected by the Conservative dominated House of Lords, who wished to force a General Election over the issue. The General Election was duly held in January 2010. The Liberal Party lost its majority, but it was able to retain power with the support of the newly emerging Labour Party and the Irish Parliamentary Party. The House of Lords then passed the People's Budget, however the price of the Irish support was that the House of Lords would be reformed, so that it could no longer block measures to give Ireland Home Rule. So another General Election was held in December 1910, which produced an almost identical result, The Liberals, again supported by Labour and the Irish sought to pass the Parliament Act 1911, which removed the Lords power to veto any money Bills and meant they could only delay the passage of other Bills passed by the Commons for up to 2 years. The Act was passed when Asquith threatened to ask King George V to create hundreds of new Liberal Lords. The National Insurance Act 1911 was then passed, introducing a health insurance scheme for workers, to which employers and government contributed.

1912

Titanic's maiden voyage from Southampton to the home of the free

Was met by an iceberg and the bottom of the sea

1912: TITANIC SINKS

During the 19th Century ships in the Royal Navy had been transformed from wooden hulled vessels with large masts, propelled by the wind, with which Nelson had won the Battle of Trafalgar in 1805, to iron hulled steamships, driven by propellers and powered by burning large quantities of coal, by the century's end. Britain was not only the strongest naval power in the world, but its determination to maintain this position was such that in 1889 Lord Salisbury's government had passed the Naval Defence Act, which required the Royal Navy to have as many battleships as at least the next two strongest naval powers combined. At that time this was France and Russia, but very soon the German Empire, which had been created by the unification of the German states under the Prussian King Wilhelm I in 1871, was to enter into a naval arms race with Britain, which focused on a new type of ship with extraordinary fire power, known as the Dreadnought.

At the same time there was a competition between civilian ship owners to create the best passenger ships, in particular to transport people across the Atlantic to the United States. As one of three "Olympic-class" ships built for the British White Star Line by Belfast shipbuilders, Harland and Wolff, the Titanic, was the largest ship in the world when it set off on its maiden voyage from Southampton to New York on 10 April 1912. Three days later it struck an iceberg and sank, killing more than 1,500 of those on board. The ship, which was 269 metres long, with 4 funnels, and 3 engines, and which had 176 men to shovel 600 tons of coal a day into its furnace, was a luxury liner. It was also built to be unsinkable, with 16 compartments and watertight doors which could seal them off individually. Unfortunately, the iceberg caused a breach in, and flooded, 5 of these, which was too many for it to stay afloat, and the lack of enough lifeboats, meant that only 710 people survived. It was the worst maritime disaster the world had experienced.

1913

Emily highlights woman's plight on Epsom course

By being downtrodden to death by the King's horse

1913: EMILY DAVISON – VOTES FOR WOMEN

The word "suffrage" comes from an old Latin word for "ballot" and has come to mean "the right to vote". The expression "universal suffrage" is used when all adults in an area are allowed to vote in free elections. Universal suffrage was finally achieved in the United Kingdom in 1928, when the Equal Franchise Act, provided that all men and women over the age of 21 were entitled to vote. This age was reduced to 18 in 1969.

Prior to 1928 there had always been restrictions on who could vote in elections. Traditionally, only those owning property over a certain value were allowed to vote, although until the Roman Catholic Relief Act in 1829, Catholics were excluded from Parliament. Before the Great Reform Act 1832 women were allowed to vote if they met the property qualifications, although in practice very few did so. That Act, while increasing the number of males that could vote, also provided, for the first time, that only males could vote. Further Reform Acts followed in 1867 and 1884, together with other measures to make ballots secret, remove corrupt practices and distribute Parliamentary seats more evenly, but throughout the 19th Century there was resistance to allowing women the right to vote, or to stand for Parliament.

Women's suffrage was a worldwide issue at the start of the 20th Century. In the United Kingdom it enjoyed widespread support, and a movement, led by Emmeline Pankhurst, known as the suffragettes, engaged in militant actions to try to force politicians to act. One leading suffragette, Emily Davison, ran out in front of a horse belonging to King George V during the Derby horse race at Epsom on 4 June 1913, and was knocked over and killed. While suffragette activities were suspended during World War One, Lloyd George's government passed the Representation of the People Act in early 1918, giving the vote to women over 30. The 1928 Act put women on equal terms with men.

1914

European powers split into opposing camps is too far gone

Archduke Ferdinand's assassination sets off World War One

1914: START OF WORLD WAR ONE

At the start of 1914, as a result of an earlier series of wars and treaties, Europe was divided into two camps. Largely in response to the growing threat posed by the German Empire, Britain and France had resolved many of their colonial disputes in 1904, in agreements known as the Entente Cordiale, and with similar agreements reached with the Russian Empire, the relationship between the three countries was known as the Triple Entente. At the same time a defensive alliance existed between the great central European powers, the German and Austria-Hungary Empires and Italy, known as the Triple Alliance.

While a great war between the two sides seemed inevitable at some stage, the events that precipitated it took place in the Balkans. Having successfully fought for independence from the Turkish Ottoman Empire in the first Balkan War in 1913, the Balkan nations then warred with one another. On 28 June 1914 Archduke Ferdinand, the heir to the Austria-Hungary Empire, was murdered in Bosnia by Serbian rebels. This led to Austria-Hungary declaring war on Serbia on 25 July. Russia, who were allies of Serbia, ordered a general mobilisation of its armed forces. As a result, Germany declared war on Russia on 1st August, and demanded that France remained neutral in any conflict. It then declared war on France on 3 August, and invaded Belgium when Belgium refused to allow free passage of the German Army across Belgium. Under the Treaty of London 1839, Britain had agreed to guarantee Belgium's neutrality in any war, and when Germany refused to withdraw from Belgium, Asquith's Government declared war on Germany on 4th August 1914 and on Austria-Hungary 8 days later. The war that followed was the first truly global war, fought principally in Europe, but also in the colonies. Other nations joining on the British side included Japan and Italy and, in 1917, the United States. Those joining Germany included the Ottoman Empire and Bulgaria.

1918

British emerge victorious from trenches everyone abhors

But would it really be the war to end all wars

1918: END OF WORLD WAR ONE

After the German Empire's failure to achieve a rapid victory over France in August 1914, the two sides dug trenches which stretched from the North Sea to Switzerland, and engaged in trench warfare for the next 4 years. Despite several massive offensives, notably the Battles of Verdun and of the Somme in 1916 and of Passchendaele in 1917, which together resulted in more than 2 million casualties, the battle lines hardly moved. Germany had more success on the Eastern Front, and after assisting the Communist Bolsheviks to overthrow the Russian Tsar in 1917, Russia, now called the Soviet Socialist Republic, left the war in early 1918. The United States, while providing support for the British side, had resisted joining the war until 1917, when they saw the opportunity to bring global warfare to an end. After German troops were released from the Eastern front, following the peace treaty with Russia, they started a major offensive in the West. This was rebuffed, and with large numbers of new American troops on the British side, the Germans were driven back and had no answer. Kaiser Wilhelm abdicated, and the fighting ended on 11 November 1918.

The war brought to an end the German, Austria-Hungary, Ottoman and Russian Empires, and led to the creation of many new nations. It was also followed by many revolutions. In the United Kingdom, the Irish fought a war of independence with the British. While Irish Republicans had been crushed in the 1916 Easter Uprising, the republican party, Sinn Fein, won most of the Irish seats in the 1918 General Election, and declared Irish Independence. Guerrilla warfare was brought to an end in 1921, when Ireland was partitioned, with the creation of the Irish Free State, and Northern Ireland remaining in the United Kingdom. While World War One had resulted in about 800,000 British and 20 million total deaths, the Spanish flu pandemic, from 1918 to 1920, killed more than 50 million worldwide, including 228,000 in Britain.

1924

A party representing workers shows that it can govern, who would have thought?

MacDonald's Labour Government wins power, with Liberal support

1924: FIRST LABOUR PRIME MINISTER

While the Liberal Party had been the party of reform, steering the country towards a more equal and democratic society, a more radical party emerged at the start of the 20th Century, which was to replace it as the main opposition to the Conservative Party from 1923 onwards. The Labour Party evolved out of various workers' rights and socialist groups, and supported by the Trade Union Congress, and an electoral pact with the Liberals, won 29 seats in the 1906 General Election, with Keir Hardie playing a leading role. It did not look back.

Ramsay MacDonald, the son of a farm labourer and a housemaid, born in Lossiemouth in Scotland in 1866, was a brilliant orator. First elected to Parliament as a Labour member in 1906, he became leader of the Party in 1911, but was forced to resign in 1914, because of his opposition to the war. In 1918 the Liberal Prime Minister, David Lloyd George, who had led a coalition government with the Conservative Party since 1916, continued that coalition into peacetime and won a huge majority in the General Election, while MacDonald lost his seat. He returned to Parliament in the 1922 General Election, when Bonar Law's Conservatives won a comfortable majority, and became leader of the Labour Party once more. The following year, when Stanley Baldwin became Conservative Party leader and Prime Minster and decided to call another General Election, MacDonald's Labour Party won more seats than the Liberals and became the Official Opposition. Although still the biggest party in the Commons, the Conservatives no longer had a majority, and, in January 1924, MacDonald was invited by King George V to form a government, with Liberal support. He was Prime Minister until November 1924, when Baldwin's Conservatives won a majority at a further General Election. In 1929 he led another minority government, with Labour winning more seats than any other party for the first time. He remained Prime Minister until 1935, and died in 1937.

1925

First public demonstration of television by John Logie Baird

The start of 24 hour entertainment and eyes that are squared

1925: FIRST PUBLIC DEMONSTRATION OF TELEVISION

Within 20 years of James Clerk Maxwell's publication, in 1865, of his theories concerning electromagnetic waves, those theories were not only proven to be correct, but equipment was devised to generate electromagnetic waves at different frequencies. A certain spectrum of such frequencies became known as "radio waves", and further equipment designed to detect, or receive these waves, at a distance from where they were transmitted, combined with the technology developed for telephones, to convert sound into an electrical signal and that back into sound again, led to the invention of the radio, which is generally credited to the Italian inventor, Guglielmo Marconi in 1894. Marconi's company was an original shareholder in the British Broadcasting Company, incorporated in 1922, which became the British Broadcasting Corporation, or the BBC, under public ownership, in 1927.

Scottish inventor, John Logie Baird, born in 1888, designed a system for converting visual images into an electrical signal and then back into a visual image on a screen, and provided the first public demonstration of a television showing moving silhouette images at Selfridges in London in 1925. In 1926 he demonstrated a television system which could show different grey tones, which was the first time one could see recognisable faces in motion. In 1928 he demonstrated the first colour television system, and also made the first transatlantic television transmission from London to New York and created the first television broadcast for the BBC. Television was first transmitted over long distances using telephone wires, but by 1929 BBC transmitters were being used to send television pictures and sound using radio waves. Baird made the first colour broadcast in 1938. He was also responsible for other inventions, including a contribution to the development of radar during World War Two. Television broadcasts were halted during the war, and Baird died shortly after their resumption, in 1946.

1928

Fleming's accidental discovery of penicillin is one of the best stories ever told

Over 200 million lives are saved when deadly bacteria is killed by mould

1928: FLEMING DISCOVERS PENICLLIN

Bacteria are tiny single-celled organisms which live in many places, including about 39 trillion in the average human body. The majority of bacteria living in humans are harmless or beneficial, assisting in such processes as food digestion. Some bacteria can be harmful and can cause sickness or death, including the bacteria responsible for pneumonia, meningitis and food poisoning. Viruses differ from bacteria in that they are not normally considered as living entities. They consist of genetic material wrapped in proteins and they reproduce themselves by infecting living cells and stealing genetic material from those cells. Some viruses are beneficial, but they are also responsible for many diseases including influenza, rabies, AIDS and the common cold. Medical science has developed many treatments to help cure or prevent diseases caused by bacteria or viruses, including antibiotics used to safely kill harmful bacteria. The father of antibiotics is considered to be the Scottish born doctor and microbiologist, Alexander Fleming, who lived from 1881 to 1955.

Fleming had worked as a bacteriologist at St Mary's Hospital in Paddington before World War One. During the war he served in the Royal Army Medical Corp, where he noticed that the antiseptics used on infected wounds of soldiers often made them worse, rather than better, because they were applied to the surface only and did not reach or kill, the bacteria infecting the tissues below. After the war he continued to research substances that could kill bacteria. In September 1928, on returning from holiday, he discovered that a bacteria culture that he had been growing in the laboratory had been accidentally contaminated with a fungus mould, which had killed it. He called the mould penicillin, and from this discovery the first antibiotics were developed. Antibiotics now save millions of lives every year. In 1945 Fleming was awarded the Nobel Prize for Medicine in recognition of his work.

1936

Edward's plans with divorcee are for Baldwin too much of a swing

Brother George gets his crown and Mrs Simpson gets his ring

INSTRUMENT OF ABDICATION

I, Edward the Eighth, of Great Britain, Ireland, and the British Dominions beyond the Seas, King, Emperor of India, do hereby declare My irrevocable determination to renounce the Throne for Myself and for My descendants, and My desire that effect should be given to this Instrument of Abdication immediately.

In token whereof I have hereunto set My hand this tenth day of December, nineteen hundred and thirty six, in the presence of the witnesses whose signatures are subscribed.

SIGNED AT
FORT BELVEDERE
IN THE PRESENCE
OF

1936: ABDICATION OF EDWARD VIII

Stanley Baldwin, who lived from 1867 to 1947, was the leading British politician of the 1920s and 30s. He served as Conservative Prime Minister briefly from May 1923 to January 1924, and then from November 1924 to June 1929. While he continued a programme of social reform, which had formerly been championed by the Liberal Party, he had to deal with difficult economic conditions, and in 1926 a nine-day General Strike organised by the Trades Union Congress. In 1929, MacDonald's Labour Party attained the most seats, and governed again with Liberal Party support. However, Labour had no effective solution to the Great Depression which followed the Stock Market Crash of 1929, and MacDonald was encouraged by King George V to form a National Government with the Conservatives and Liberals in 1931. Baldwin then served as MacDonald's Deputy Prime Minister until 1935, and as Prime Minister again from 1935 to 1937.

Baldwin had to deal with the constitutional crisis that followed the succession to the throne of George V's son, who became King Edward VIII in 1936, after the death of his father. As Prince of Wales, since 1911, Edward had enjoyed popularity at home and abroad, however he was considered reckless by his father and politicians such as Baldwin, due to his romantic affairs with several married women. In November 1936 he informed Baldwin of his intention to marry the American Mrs Wallis Simpson, who was in the process of divorcing her second husband. Baldwin, supported by the Archbishop of Canterbury, who argued that as head of the Church of England the King could not marry a divorcee, and by the leaders of Canada, Australia and other Dominion Governments of the British Empire, forced Edward to choose Mrs Simpson or the throne. He abdicated on 11 December 1936 in favour of his brother, who became King George VI. Edward became the Duke of Windsor and married Wallis Simpson in 1937. He died in France in 1972.

1939

*When Hitler invades Poland Britain
starts to fight Germany anew*

*The Americans don't know it yet,
but it's going to be a world war too*

1939: START OF WORLD WAR TWO

When World War One ended it was followed by the creation of the League of Nations in 1920, an organisation of nations, whose purpose was to maintain world peace. It failed in this mission, principally because of the rise of extreme nationalistic movements who sought to dominate what they considered were lesser nations and peoples. In Germany, Adolf Hitler and the Nazi Party took advantage of poor economic conditions and a German desire to recover from the humiliation of defeat in World War One, and the terms that were imposed on it afterwards, to seize power in 1933, and then rebuilt Germany to a mighty industrial and military power. Mussolini, and his similar fascist movement, took over Italy in 1922. General Franco won the Spanish Civil War in 1939 and ruled as a Nationalist Dictator. The Japanese sought to dominate Asia, and invaded China in 1937. In the Soviet Union, Josef Stalin was a ruthless Dictator, with ambitions to expand Soviet control and Communism around the World.

As Germany rapidly re-armed under Hitler and aggressively sought to expand its territory, annexing Austria in 1938, Britain's Prime Minister from 1937, Neville Chamberlain, adopted a policy of appeasement towards Hitler and in 1938 signed the Munich Agreement with him, allowing Hitler to take over part of Czechoslovakia and which Chamberlain claimed had achieved "Peace for our time". But Hitler continued, invading the rest of Czechoslovakia in early 1939. When Hitler threated Poland, Britain and France pledged to guarantee its independence. However, Hitler signed a secret non-aggression pact with Stalin and invaded Poland, causing Britain and France to declare war on 3rd September 1939. The war rapidly escalated around the world, with Germany taking over most of Europe, including France, and forming the Axis Alliance with Italy and Japan. America joined the war on the British Allied side in 1941, after Japan bombed Pearl Harbour.

1940

Winston's speeches inspire troops on beaches

But silence brings victory, history teaches

1940: WINSTON CHURCHILL

Winston Churchill, born at his family home, Blenheim Palace, near Oxford, in 1874, was the son of the politician, Lord Randolph Churchill. He joined the British Army in 1893 and served in different conflicts around the British Empire, including the Boer War in 1899, where he was famously captured and escaped. His Parliamentary career began with his election as a Conservative MP in 1900. While a committed Imperialist, Churchill was a social liberal, and switched to the Liberal Party in 1904. He played a major part in the welfare reforms of the Liberal Government from 1906, becoming Home Secretary in 1910. He became First Lord of the Admiralty in 1911, and in this position was responsible, in 1915, for a disastrous assault on Gallipoli during World War One. Under Lloyd George he was Secretary of State for War and then the Colonies before losing his seat in the 1922 Election. He did not agree with the Liberals supporting MacDonald's Labour Government, and switched back to the Conservative Party, returning to Parliament in 1924, and serving as Baldwin's Chancellor of the Exchequer from 1924 to 1929. He remained an MP but was out of government from 1929 to 1939. Known as Churchill's wilderness years, it was during this period that he vocally opposed the policy of appeasement towards Hitler. He was re-appointed as First Lord of the Admiralty by Neville Chamberlain on the day Britain declared war in September 1939. As Germany swept through Europe, Chamberlain was forced to resign. Churchill and Lord Halifax, who wanted to negotiate peace terms with Hitler, were the two candidates for Prime Minister, and Churchill was appointed by King George VI, in 1940, after famously not giving an answer to the King's question as to whether he would serve under Halifax. Churchill became a great war time leader, inspiring the nation with his speeches and refusal to contemplate surrender. He was to serve as Prime Minister until 1945, and again from 1951 to 1955. A prolific and brilliant writer, he was awarded the Nobel Prize in Literature in 1953. He died in 1965.

1945

*The war is won when allied forces
overwhelm German defenders*

*And an atomic bomb is dropped on
Hiroshima and Japan surrenders*

1945: END OF WORLD WAR TWO

When Churchill became Prime Minister, in May 1940, he firstly oversaw the successful evacuation of 338,226 British and allied servicemen fleeing the German advance, from Dunkirk in Northern France, using a flotilla of more than 800 ships of all sizes, and then the victory over the German Luftwaffe by the Royal Air Force in a 16 week intensive air campaign by Hitler from July 1940, which was intended to achieve dominance over British skies as a prelude to a full scale invasion, which Churchill called the Battle of Britain, while the constant bombings of British cities, known as the Blitz, continued until May 1941.

Japan formed the Axis powers pact with Germany and Italy, in September 1940, and by the end of 1940, with most of Europe controlled by Axis forces, the British Empire started a counter offensive in Northern Africa, which the Germans, under General Rommel, drove back. Feeling that Western Europe was under stable control, Germany invaded Stalin's Soviet Union in June 1941, and Japan launched a surprise attack on the American fleet, moored in Pearl Harbour in Hawaii, in December 1941, which resulted in both the Soviet Union and the United States joining the war on the British Allied side. All-out war was now truly global.

The Axis powers early successes were being turned around by 1943. The Allies followed success in North Africa with the invasion of Italy from the South from July 1943, and in June 1944, with the D-Day landings in Normandy, the liberation of France had begun. Hitler became besieged from all sides, as the Soviet Union forces regained territory on the eastern front. They marched into Berlin in April 1945, Hitler committed suicide, and the war in Europe ended on 8 May 1945. While Japan was also in retreat, they refused to surrender until the United States dropped atomic bombs on their cities of Hiroshima and Nagasaki in August 1945. The worst conflict in human history was finally at an end.

1947

To a Commonwealth of Nations there is a transition

India gains its independence but with a partition

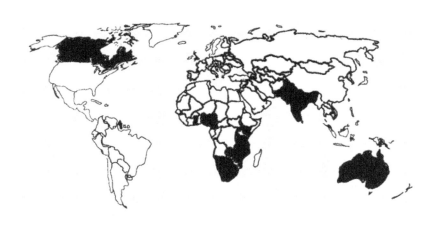

1947: INDIA INDEPENDENCE

Having served as Churchill's deputy in the wartime coalition government, Clement Attlee secured a surprising victory in the July 1945 General Election, and for the first time the Labour Party held a majority in the House of Commons. Attlee was committed to the principle that peoples and nations should be allowed to govern themselves, and he was the principal architect of the decolonisation of the British Empire.

The process of creating self-governing regions of the British Empire had begun in 1856, with 4 Australian states. Canada was granted Dominion status in 1867, and this was followed by a newly united Commonwealth of Australia in 1901, New Zealand in 1907, South Africa in 1910 and the Irish Free State in 1922. The Statute of Westminster in 1931 removed Britain's power to pass laws for the Dominions. In 1947 Attlee's government gave India its independence. In an effort to avoid conflict between Hindus and Muslims, the country was partitioned into 2 self-governing Dominions, India and Pakistan.

The Commonwealth of Nations was formally created by the London Declaration in 1949 as a free association of independent nations with shared values of democracy, human rights and the rule of law. In addition to the Dominions, apart from Ireland, most countries who attained their independence from Britain in the succeeding years remained as members of the Commonwealth, including Sri Lanka (1948), Ghana and Malaysia (1957), Nigeria (1960), Cyprus, Sierra Leone and Tanzania (1961), Jamaica, Trinidad and Uganda (1962), Kenya (1963), Malawi, Malta and Zambia (1964), Singapore, Guyana and Botswana (1966) and others. The monarch of the United Kingdom remains the monarch of 16 of the member states, as well as head of the Commonwealth, in which today live a third of the world's population.

1948

*Bevan launches a National Service
for health*

*And free medical care for all
regardless of wealth*

1948: NATIONAL HEALTH SERVICE

The creation of a universal state health service, free to all at the point of delivery, had been the policy of the Labour Party since 1934. In the Second World War the sacrifices of ordinary people led to cross party support for this idea, together with other social welfare reforms. In 1942 the Liberal, William Beveridge, produced a report for the Government called "Social Insurance and Allied Services", known as the Beveridge Report, in which he proposed sweeping reforms to address "want, disease, ignorance, squalor and idleness", which included the introduction of comprehensive health services. The Conservative Health Minister, Henry Willink, published a paper on a national health service in 1944, and with the election of Attlee's Labour Party in 1945 the idea was put into effect, together with other recommendations of the Beveridge Report, to create what we now call the welfare state. Attlee's government brought public utilities and large industries into State ownership, a process known as nationalisation, greatly expanded public services, and produced a comprehensive social security system with the National Insurance and National Assistance Acts of 1946.

Attlee gave the task of creating the National Health Service to the Welsh MP, Aneurin Bevan, who was made the Minister of Health in 1945. The service was created by the National Health Service Act 1946, which came into force on 5th July 1948, when 2,688 local authority and charity hospitals came under central state control and ownership. The service had 3 core principles: to be universal, free and based on clinical need not the ability to pay. Henceforth all citizens of the United Kingdom, who needed it, could freely attain, at any time, medical treatment and advice, including dental treatment. Later on some of the huge cost of this service would be defrayed by the introduction of prescription and other charges, but in general the NHS has remained true to its original ideals and enjoys widespread popular support.

1952

When the young Queen came to the throne the people got more than they reckoned

Britain's longest reigning monarch, Elizabeth the Second

1952: ELIZABETH II

When Elizabeth Windsor was born in London on 21 April 1926, the first child of the Duke of York, who was King George V's second son, it was not expected that she would succeed to the throne. In 1936 George V died. His first son became King Edward VIII but abdicated in the same year. Elizabeth's father then became King George VI. George VI was to have only one other child, a daughter called Margaret, who was born in 1930. At that time, and until the law was changed by the Succession to the Crown Act 2013, a male child would have preceded an older sister in the line of succession, however as George VI had no sons when he died, at the age of 56, in 1952, Elizabeth became Queen Elizabeth II.

Elizabeth was only 25 when she became the monarch of the United Kingdom and other nations within the Commonwealth. In 1947, in a radio broadcast to the people of the Commonwealth, she had pledged to devote the whole of her life to their service. In the same year she had married Prince Philip of Greece and Denmark, who was made the Duke of Edinburgh, and who adopted the surname of Mountbatten. Elizabeth was however to retain the surname of Windsor, which thus remains the name of the royal house. They had 4 children, Charles, born in 1948, who was to become the Prince of Wales on her succession in 1952, followed by Anne (1950), Andrew (1960) and Edward (1964).

Elizabeth's first Prime Minister was Winston Churchill, who had returned to power after defeating Attlee in the 1951 General Election. Her Coronation, held in Westminster Abbey on 2 June 1953, was the first to be shown live on television. While her reign has seen many changes, Elizabeth has been a model constitutional monarch and Head of the Commonwealth. In 2015 she became the longest reigning British monarch, surpassing her great-great-grandmother, Queen Victoria.

1953

Crick and Watson win the Nobel prize one day

For life changing discoveries about the DNA

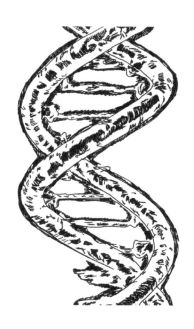

1953: STRUCTURE OF DNA DISCOVERED

Charles Darwin's theory of evolution, first published in 1859, provided an explanation for how and why different life forms changed over time and in different environments, based on the observation that there were slight variations in all organisms, and that those variations which most aided survival, such as, for example, a bird having a slightly smaller beak finding it easier to get food in a particular environment, were then passed down to offspring. The search to explain how such chance variations occurred in the first place, led to the development of genetic science and to the discovery that such variations were caused by genetic mutations.

Englishman, Francis Crick, and American, James Watson, were notable pioneers in this area, who working together at the Cavendish Laboratory in Cambridge, discovered the structure of deoxyribonucleic acid, or DNA, in 1953, for which work they were awarded the Nobel Prize in Medicine in 1962. DNA is found in all living cells and consists of two long chains which twist around one another in a double helix. Each paired chain is made of millions of what are called bases, with each base being composed of one of 4 substances, which are referred to as C, G, A and T. It is the sequence of these bases, and their position in the chain as a whole, which forms the genetic code for living things. A gene is simply a section of the DNA chain that corresponds to some trait, such as the colour of a creature's eyes. In every human cell there are 46 DNA chains, known as chromosomes, which are paired, with each parent contributing one chromosome in each pair. One of these 46 chromosomes, always provided by the male parent, determines the sex. When cells multiply, all of the DNA chains, or chromosomes, are duplicated in each new cell, but occasionally this does not happen perfectly, and thus the genetic code is slightly different. This is how genetic mutations occur, and evolution is possible.

1956

At the core of the world's first nuclear plant in Calder Hall

Are the atom splitting chain reactions which may destroy us all.

1956: FIRST NUCLEAR POWER STATION

At the end of World War Two, in 1945, the winning allied nations, including the United Kingdom, created the United Nations, an intergovernmental organisation intended to help preserve peace and promote human rights. Its greatest challenge was that its two most powerful members, the democratic United States and the communist Soviet Union, who had replaced Nazi control of Eastern European countries with its own, were entirely ideologically opposed. The Cold War had begun. The North Atlantic Treaty Organisation, or NATO, was created as a system of mutual defence by Western nations in 1949, and the Soviet Union responded with the creation of the Warsaw Pact consisting of communist Eastern states in 1955. Both sides started to rapidly develop nuclear weapons of incredible power, in a nuclear arms race, which meant that neither side could afford to directly attack the other; maintaining a peace based on what was called mutual assured destruction. This did not prevent indirect conflicts, such as the Korean War from 1950 to 1953 and the Vietnam War from 1955 to 1975.

The basis of atomic weapons was the discovery that atoms have enormous quantities of energy locked up within them, and that this energy could be released by splitting the atom by bombarding it with neutrons. The splitting of the atom, usually of uranium, released further neutrons, which in turn split more atoms, leading to a chain reaction, and a massive energy burst. In a bomb this was allowed to occur in an uncontrolled fashion, but it was also discovered that one could slow down the reaction, which meant one could harness the energy to heat water, and generate electricity using a steam turbine. The world's first commercial nuclear power station was opened at Calder Hall, at Windscale in England in 1956. Nuclear power generates very significant energy from a small amount of uranium, without the pollution one gets from burning coal or oil, but at great cost if something goes wrong.

1962

The 1960s are peppered with songs from the band

Such as all you need is love and I want to hold your hand

1962: THE BEATLES

The 1960s was a period of enormous social and cultural change in Britain. The post war period had been one of austerity and rebuilding, with food rationing only ending in 1954, and Britain's influence and power in the world rapidly declining. Churchill's Conservatives had returned to Government in 1951, with his deputy, Anthony Eden, replacing him as Prime Minister in 1955. But following the Suez Crisis in 1956, when Britain humiliatingly failed to regain control of the Suez Canal in Egypt, Eden resigned. He was followed as Prime Minister by Harold Macmillan in 1957, and then by Sir Alec Douglas-Home in 1963. But in 1964, after 13 years of Conservative Party rule, Harold Wilson's Labour Party won the election, and embarked on an ambitious programme of liberal social reforms, which included legalising abortion and homosexuality and abolishing the death penalty.

The decade became known as the swinging 60s, because in a period of relative prosperity, the newly introduced birth control pill, and an emphasis on art, fashion and music, the young had never enjoyed so much freedom. Britain, and London in particular, led worldwide cultural change. Popular music was at the forefront of this, with British bands such as the Rolling Stones, the Who and the Kinks dominating music charts around the world. One band who stood out above all the rest was the Beatles, led by Paul McCartney and John Lennon, from Liverpool. Formed in 1960, the band revolutionised popular music with their innovations and combination of musical styles. After their first hit record in 1962, they went on to be the most successful band of all time, producing albums such as *Sargent Pepper's Lonely Heart Club Band* and *Abbey Road.* When the band broke up, in 1970, its 4 members each enjoyed successful solo careers. John Lennon, who had been active in the peace movement protesting nuclear weapons and the Vietnam War, was murdered outside of his New York home in 1980.

1973

With Common Market membership the UK joins the European project

If it later progresses to a European Union who could possibly object

1973: JOINING THE EUROPEAN COMMON MARKET

In the 1950s, starting with the European Coal and Steel Community created by the Treaty of Paris in 1951, major European powers, such as France, West Germany and Italy, moved towards economic and political union with the aim of increasing prosperity and preventing further war. In 1957 they established the European Economic Community, also known as the Common Market, initially with 6 members. In 1961 the United Kingdom, led by Harold Macmillan's Conservative Government, applied to join, but was refused entry by France's President De Gaulle, who feared the very close relationship between the United States and Britain would be detrimental to the Community. A further application was made by Harold Wilson's Labour Government in 1967, and when the Conservatives regained power, under Edward Heath, in 1970, his Government successfully negotiated membership, with the United Kingdom joining on 1 January 1973, at the same time as Ireland.

The decimalisation of the British currency, which occurred in 1971, was seen as a step towards entry into the Common Market. Until that date, and since Roman times, a pound, originally of silver, was divided into 240 pence. There were 12 old pence in a shilling, and 20 shillings made a pound. After 1971 a pound consisted of 100 new pence.

Entry into the Common Market was not universally popular in Britain, particularly as it meant a significant weakening of Britain's ties with the Commonwealth countries. It was however supported by two thirds of people voting in a referendum in 1975. This was the first national referendum ever to be held in Britain, and had been promised by Wilson in the two general elections held in 1974. The first, in February, had returned Labour to power but without a majority; the second in October gave Wilson a small majority. The European Community was to continue to develop, becoming the European Union in 1993.

1979

People punish Labour for winter of discontent

And number one lady to number 10 is sent

1979: FIRST FEMALE PRIME MINISTER

Margaret Thatcher was born Margaret Roberts in Grantham, Lincolnshire in 1925. She studied Chemistry at Oxford University, and was to become not only the United Kingdom's first woman Prime Minister, but also the first with a Science degree. Graduating in 1947, she worked as a research Chemist for several years before training in the law and becoming a barrister in 1953. She stood as a Conservative candidate 3 times unsuccessfully from 1950, before being elected as the Member of Parliament for Finchley in 1959. She was given a junior position in Macmillan's government in 1961, and continued to progress when the Conservatives were in opposition to Wilson's Labour Government between 1964 and 1970, being appointed Shadow Secretary of State for Education and Science in 1967, and then holding that position in Government after Edward Heath won the 1970 general election. During the 1960s she was an ardent critic of Labour's high taxation policies and a strong supporter of free market economics.

As Education Secretary, Thatcher sought to slow down the movement towards non-selective Comprehensive Secondary Schools, which had started in 1946, and which were rapidly replacing the old system of Grammar Schools, for the more able students, and Secondary Modern Schools for the rest.

After Heath's Government struggled with the unions and an energy crisis, which led to a three-day working week in 1973 to conserve electricity, Labour returned to power in 1974, and Thatcher replaced Heath as leader of the Conservative Party in 1975. James Callaghan took over from Wilson as Labour leader and Prime Minister in 1976. In the face of severe economic problems and strikes, and what became known as the winter of discontent, Callaghan lost the 1979 General Election and Thatcher became Prime Minister with a 44-seat majority.

1982

After leader looks for popularity boost in the South Atlantic arena

British take back the Falklands Islands in a fight with Argentina

1982: FALKLANDS WAR

In the decade leading up to Margaret Thatcher's election in 1979 the United Kingdom had been regularly referred to as the "sick man of Europe" in reference to the frequent worker strikes over pay and its poor economic performance compared to other European countries. At that time the inflation rate was rapidly increasing, with average prices in 1980 being some 16% higher than the year before. High inflation led to high wage increase demands and strikes, and Thatcher identified bringing inflation down as the most important factor in turning the economy around. To achieve this, she increased interest rates and taxes and curtailed public spending. By 1982 inflation had been brought down to 8% and an economic recovery was starting, but unemployment had rocketed to more than 3 million. While Thatcher was a resolute politician who relished in her nickname as "the iron lady", her popularity was then at a low ebb.

Another Government that was looking to increase its popularity, in the face of grave economic difficulties and civil protests, was the military junta that had ruled Argentina since 1976. In April 1982 they chose to try to enforce a long-standing Argentine claim to sovereignty over the Falkland Islands, which were situated nearly 1,000 miles away from them in the South Atlantic, by invading them. The Falkland Islands had been a British Crown colony since 1833, and had a population of 1,820 people, mostly of British descent. Thatcher launched a naval task force to retake the islands, and received the support of the United Nations Security Council, the Commonwealth and the European Community. The islands were successfully recaptured after a 10-week war. In 1983, the junta fell, Argentina returned to democracy and Thatcher rode a wave of new popularity to victory in the general election. In 1984, Thatcher agreed to the transfer of Britain's most important remaining colony, Hong Kong, to China in 1997, ending 156 years of British rule.

1989

Use of the internet explodes as the World Wide Web is invented by Tim Berners-Lee

Communications and access to information are revolutionised, globalised and free.

1989: THE WORLD WIDE WEB

From the time that Michael Faraday discovered the principles of electromagnetic induction in 1831, the remarkable properties of electricity continued to be discovered and exploited to create the modern world. Electricity was not only a highly convenient medium for conveying energy and communications over a long distance, it could also be used to generate electromagnetic waves, which, at different frequencies, we now call radio waves, x-rays, microwaves and light. It could also be used to lay down patterns on magnetic tape, making audio and video recording possible, and tiny amounts of electrical charge can be stored in, what became, miniscule transistors, now usually made of silicon, making computers possible. The term digital is used to describe data stored in zeros and ones, and a single memory cell or transistor can be considered to be one or the other depending on whether it is holding an electrical charge or not. Computers work by converting information into a binary number or code, and having a vast amount of memory cells to store it in. This is why computers are described as digital technology, and we are said to live in a digital age.

The English mathematician, Alan Turing, born in 1912, was the father of computer science and artificial intelligence. Working at Bletchley Park, Turing was responsible for cracking German radio code messages in World War Two, and afterwards he created the Automatic Computing Engine. The development of the silicon microcomputer chip, holding greater and greater quantities of ever smaller transistors, led to vast computer memory operating at faster speeds. Aside from computers, computer chips are now found in everything from mobile phones to toasters. The internet was first created in the 1960s, with the launch of connections between different computer networks. In 1989 the English computer scientist, Timothy Berners-Lee invented the world wide web, making global internet communication available to everyone.

1990

Maggie's out, Major's in
Howe's that man who made him win

1990: THATCHER OUT, MAJOR IN

Margaret Thatcher held power from 1979 to 1990, and was the longest serving Prime Minister of the 20th Century. A year after her landslide victory in the 1983 Election, she nearly followed Spencer Perceval, who was assassinated in 1812, to became the second British Prime Minister to be murdered in office, when the IRA bombed the Grand Hotel in Brighton, where she was staying while attending the 1984 Conservative Party Conference. She survived and went on to see off a year long strike by the National Union of Mineworkers, and with an economy growing, unemployment and inflation coming down, and a promise of lower taxes, she won another landslide victory in the 1987 Election. In both the 1983 and 1987 elections she was greatly assisted by a split in the Labour Party which had occurred in 1981, with the formation of a new centrist political party, called the Social Democratic Party or SDP. The SDP formed an electoral alliance with the Liberal Party, and this alliance nearly succeeded in getting more votes than Labour in both elections. In 1988 the 2 parties merged to become the Liberal Democratic Party.

Thatcher came under fire from her own party in her third term for introducing the short lived and widely unpopular Community Charge, which was dubbed the "Poll Tax", and was then forced to resign after being attacked by her former Deputy, Geoffrey Howe, for her opposition to greater European integration. She was succeeded as Prime Minister by her Chancellor, John Major. Major's Government then agreed to the Maastrict Treaty in 1992, which led to the European Community being replaced by the European Union, or EU, in 1993. The EU constituted a far greater political union of the member states, and led to the creation of a single currency, known as the Euro, for many of them, which the UK did not adopt. Major also secured for himself another 5 years as Prime Minister, by winning the 1992 Election, with a slim majority. Thatcher was made a Baroness in 1992 and died in 2013.

1997

Paris crash, it can't be true

Dodi do die, Di do die too

1997: DIANA'S DEATH

Eighteen years of Conservative Party rule came to an end in May 1997, when Scottish born, Tony Blair, who had led the Labour Party since 1994, won the General Election, with a large majority. Since the last Labour Government in 1979 there had been significant rolling back of Socialism. The Thatcher and Major governments had sought to reduce taxation and to increase private ownership by encouraging Council tenants to buy their own homes and embarking on a massive programme of denationalisation. British industry sold back to private investors included British Petroleum, Rolls Royce, British Aerospace, British Gas, British Airways, British Steel, British Telecom, British Rail, British Coal, water and electricity companies, and many others. Socialism was also in retreat abroad, as the Communist Soviet Union had collapsed in 1991 and the East European countries it controlled up to 1989 had all swiftly removed their Communist Governments, including East Germany, which reunited with West Germany in 1991. Tony Blair embraced the movement away from Socialism, abandoning the Labour Party's commitment to nationalisation and high taxation, and seizing the centre ground, with what he called New Labour.

One of the first things that Blair had to deal with on taking office was the death of Diana, Princess of Wales, in a car crash in Paris on 31 August 1997. Born Diana Spencer in 1961, she married Prince Charles in St Pauls Cathedral in 1981. They had two children, William and Harry, born in 1982 and 1984, but it had not been a happy marriage, and they had separated in 1992, and divorced in 1996. Diana was enormously popular, both in Britain and abroad. She was noted for her charity work, particularly with AIDS victims, and her campaign to eradicate landmines. Her sudden death, together with her friend Dodi Fayed, shocked the world. Called the "People's Princess" by Blair, her televised funeral at Westminster Abbey was seen by 2.5 billion people worldwide.

1998

Northern Ireland resolves its troubles with a power sharing accord

Good Friday Agreement persuades Republicans and Unionists to lay down the sword

1998: THE GOOD FRIDAY AGREEMENT

The island of Ireland had been partitioned into two regions in 1920, when 6 of the 9 counties of the province of Ulster became Northern Ireland, and the rest of Ireland became Southern Ireland. While most of the people living in Southern Ireland were Catholic and supported Irish independence, the majority of the those living in Northern Ireland were Protestant, and of British descent, and wished to remain in the United Kingdom. Accordingly, when the Irish Free State was established in 1922, the Northern Ireland Parliament opted out. But a significant minority of those living in Northern Ireland were Catholic, and the Irish Republican Army, or IRA, which had played a major role in the war for independence, continued to garner support, and there was regular unrest. In the late 1960s, a campaign to improve the civil rights of Catholics, who were severely discriminated against, turned into extreme violence and the period known as the Troubles began. In 1972 thirteen unarmed Catholic protestors were killed by British soldiers in what became known as Bloody Sunday, and the Northern Ireland Parliament was suspended. In the effective civil war between republican nationalists and unionists many atrocities were committed, and more than 3,500 people were killed. After years of efforts to try to resolve the conflict the two sides finally came to a peace agreement, known as the Good Friday Agreement, in 1998. This agreement provided for power sharing between the two communities in a new Northern Ireland Assembly at Stormont, the decommissioning of arms, and, significantly, an agreement by Ireland to give up its constitutional claim to jurisdiction over Northern Ireland, but on condition that Northern Ireland would be reunited with Ireland if in the future there was majority support for this on both sides of the border. As a result, the IRA declared an end to its campaign in 2005, and the political party which had supported it, Sinn Fein, became part of the devolved government, together with the Democratic Unionist Party, in 2007.

1999

New Scottish and Welsh Parliaments established after referendum

If people want to exercise devolved powers we now know where to send them

1999: SCOTTISH AND WELSH PARLIAMENTS

While England and Wales have shared their law and legal systems for centuries, when Scotland joined the United Kingdom, with the Acts of Union in 1707, it retained its own law and distinctive legal system. As a result it was often necessary for the United Kingdom Parliament to pass laws which only applied to Scotland, and the practice developed of such legislation being considered by a Scottish Grand Committee, consisting of all of the Scottish MPs, before being finally decided by the UK Parliament as a whole. The 20th Century saw a growing demand for some form of home rule in Scotland. The Conservatives, whose full official name is the Conservative and Unionist Party, were generally opposed to this, but Labour were generally sympathetic. Support for the two parties had been evenly split in Scotland in the 1950s, but from the 1964 election Scotland became a power base for Labour. In 1979 Labour organised a referendum in Scotland to see whether there was support for a Scottish Assembly, but less than a third of registered voters voted for it. A similar assembly in Wales was supported by only 12% of voters in a referendum there.

In the 18 years of Conservative rule, from 1979, the Scottish Nationalist Party, or SNP, had seen a growth in support. The SNP campaigned for Scottish independence. It had originally been a right-wing party when it was founded in 1934, and it had opposed Britain joining the European Community in 1973. However, it moved to the centre-left and became pro-European, and now constituted a considerable threat to Labour. In winning the 1997 Election, Tony Blair's Labour Party promised new referendums in Scotland and Wales. These occurred in 1998. In Scotland the vote was a decisive "yes", in Wales "yes" won by a very narrow margin. In 1999 a Scottish Parliament and a Welsh Assembly, together with Scottish and Welsh Executives, later to be called governments, were created with devolved powers in many areas.

21st CENTURY

The 21st Century sees computers, artificial intelligence and robotics lead the way

A revolution on a global scale, but at what cost is hard to say

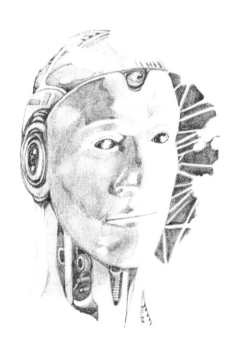

21st CENTURY (2001 to 2100)

Monarchs of Great Britain and Northern Ireland

Elizabeth II   1952-   Windsor

Prime Ministers of Great Britain and Northern Ireland

Tony Blair   1997-2007   Labour
Gordon Brown   2007-2010   Labour
David Cameron   2010-2016   Conservative
Theresa May   2016-2019   Conservative
Boris Johnson   2019-   Conservative

2003

Saddam ousted as weapons of mass destruction cause war in the Middle East

According to Blair's sexed up dossier they should have found some at least

2003: SECOND GULF WAR

In his first term as Prime Minister, from 1997 to 2001, Tony Blair had introduced significant reforms. In addition to the establishment of devolved parliaments and governments in Scotland, Wales and Northern Ireland, he limited the number of hereditary lords who could sit in the House of Lords to 92, passed the Human Rights Act and introduced a national minimum hourly wage. Blair was popular, and the Labour Party enjoyed another landslide victory in the June 2001 General Election. However, on 11th September 2001, the Islamic militant group, known a Al-Qaeda, led by Osama bin Laden, hijacked 4 passenger airliners in the United States and flew aircraft into both of the Twin Towers of the World Trade Centre in New York, and into the US military headquarters, the Pentagon, near Washington. This event caused Blair to now focus on the threat posed by such groups, in what was called "the War on Terror". He committed British Forces to join the United States, and other allies, in a war in Afghanistan, where Al-Qaeda had its main base, and support from the Taliban government.

Blair also joined the United States in its invasion of Iraq in 2003. This was known as the second Gulf war. The first Gulf War, in 1991, had followed Iraq's invasion of the neighbouring country of Kuwait. This had been repulsed by an international coalition, including the UK, but had left the dictator Saddam Hussein still in power in Iraq. In 2003 it was falsely alleged that Saddam had allied himself with Al-Qaeda, and it was believed that he held what were called weapons of mass destruction, consisting of chemical, biological or nuclear weapons which posed a significant threat to Britain and other countries. Blair supported the United States' President Bush's decision to remove Saddam, and a dossier was drawn up to persuade Parliament and the public of the threat posed. Iraq was invaded, and Saddam was ousted. However, the alleged weapons of mass destruction were never found.

WHAT HAPPENED NEXT?

What happened after 2003? Here is a quick year by year summary:

2004 The UK Independence Party, who campaigned for the UK to leave the European Union, made gains in the European Parliament Election. In that election the Conservatives won 27 of the UK seats, Labour 19, UKIP 12, Liberal Democrats 12, Green 2 and SNP 2. Labour also performed poorly in local government elections. Tony Blair announced that he would resign as Prime Minister during the next Parliament, if Labour won the next General Election. A new Scottish Parliament Building at Holyrood in Edinburgh was opened. Great Britain finished 10th in the medal count at the Summer Olympics in Athens.

2005 Prince Charles married Camilla Parker Bowles, who became HRH The Duchess of Cornwall. Tony Blair's Labour Party won third General Election in a row, with reduced majority of 66 seats, and the Democratic Unionist Party became the biggest party in Northern Ireland. In that election Labour won 355 seats, Conservatives 198, Liberal Democrats 62, DUP 9 and SNP 6. London was chosen to host the 2012 Olympic Games. On 7th July three bombs were exploded on London Underground trains and one on a London bus by Islamic suicide bombers, killing 52 people and injuring more than 700. The IRA announced an end to its armed campaign. David Cameron was elected as leader of the Conservative Party, replacing Michael Howard. The Civil Partnership Act allowed same-sex couples similar rights to married heterosexuals.

2006   A new chamber for the National Assembly of Wales, the Senedd, opened in Cardiff. Menzies Campbell elected leader of Liberal Democrats. Warmest year on record in the UK.

2007   The DUP and Sinn Fein, the two largest parties in Northern Ireland, reached agreement on power sharing. Devolved powers restored to the Northern Ireland Assembly at Stormont, and DUP leader Ian Paisley became First Minister of Northern Ireland, and Sinn Fein's Martin McGuinness deputy First Minister. SNP became the biggest party in the Scottish Parliament election, and form a minority Scottish government under Alex Salmond. Tony Blair stood down, replaced by Gordon Brown as Labour Party leader and Prime Minister. A smoking ban was imposed in all inside public places in England. Nick Clegg elected leader of Liberal Democrats.

2008   A financial crisis which began in the USA, caused by banks lending money without sufficient security, spread across the world. To prevent British banks from collapse the Chancellor of the Exchequer, Alistair Darling, introduced a £500 billion rescue package. Conservative Boris Johnston elected Mayor of London. Great Britain was 4th in the medal table at Olympic Games in Beijing, behind China, USA and Russia. The size of the British economy shrinks for the first time since 1992.

2009   Global financial crisis continued. The Bank of England reduced the interest rate for borrowing to the lowest level in its history, at 0.5%. Unemployment rose to highest level since 1994. Economy continued to shrink. Many MPs found to have overclaimed Parliamentary expenses. Far-right British National Party won 2 seats in the European Parliament election. United Kingdom Supreme Court replaced the Judicial Committee of the House of Lords as the final court of appeal.

2010   David Cameron's Conservatives won most seats in General Election, but were 20 seats short of a majority. Gordon Brown resigned as Prime Minister and was replaced by Cameron, who formed a Coalition Government with Nick Clegg's Liberal Democratic Party. The Green Party won its first seat in Parliament. In that election the Conservatives won 306 seats, Labour 258, Liberal Democrats 57 and SNP 6. Ed Miliband was elected leader of the Labour Party. Government started making large reductions in public spending. Unemployment fell. The Equality Act came into force.

2011 Welsh voted to give the Welsh Assembly more powers. Prince William married Catherine Middleton in Westminster Abbey, the couple becoming the Duke and Duchess of Cambridge. Alex Salmon's SNP wins a majority of seats in Scottish Parliament Election. Labour win half the seats in the Welsh Assembly Election. Voters reject a reform of the electoral system in a referendum. Protests against budget cuts and austerity. Riots in English Cities led to Parliament being recalled during the Summer. Mandatory retirement age abolished.

2012 Queen Elizabeth II celebrated 60 years on the throne in her Diamond Jubilee year. Boris Johnson re-elected as London Mayor. Labour and SNP did well in local elections. London hosted the Summer Olympic Games and Britain came third in the medal table, behind USA and China. Prime Minister David Cameron and Scottish First Minister Alex Salmond agreed to hold a referendum on Scottish independence. Levenson Report on media practices and ethics was highly critical, and recommended reforms. England had wettest year on record.

2013 The Marriage (Same Sex Couples) Act passed by Parliament, allowing same sex marriage from 2014 in England and Wales. Prince George is born to the Duke and Duchess of Cambridge, becoming third in line to the throne. Church of England agreed to allow women to be bishops.

2014 Nigel Farage's UK Independence Party won more UK votes and seats than any other party in the European Parliament Election. Scottish people voted against Scottish independence in referendum. SNP leader Alex Salmond resigned, and his deputy, Nicola Sturgeon, succeeded him unopposed, and became First Minister of Scotland. Three Conservative MPs defected to UKIP, and two resigned their seats and were re-elected as UKIP MPs in by-elections. It was the warmest year in the UK since records began.

2015 Cross party agreement signed to tackle climate change and to end coal burning for power. The rate of inflation fell to zero for the first time. David Cameron's Conservatives promised a referendum on the UK's membership of the European Union and won a small majority in General Election and he remained as Prime Minister. The Liberal Democrats, his former Coalition partners, led by the former Deputy Prime Minister, Nick Clegg, were nearly wiped out. The SNP won all but three of the seats in Scotland. In that election the Conservatives won 331 seats, Labour 232, SNP 56, Liberal Democrats 8, DUP 8 and UKIP 1. Ed Miliband resigned as Labour Leader and Jeremy Corbyn was elected by the party to replace him, becoming Leader of the Opposition. Tim Farron was elected to replace Nick Clegg as leader of the Liberal Democrats. A group called Islamic State had taken over a large part of Iraq and Syria, and Parliament voted for air strikes against them in Syria. Last deep coal mine was closed. There was considerable flooding in Northern England.

2016 Arlene Foster was elected leader of the DUP and became Northern Ireland's First Minister. A new National Living Wage was introduced. Sadiq Khan was elected as Mayor of London.

His predecessor, Boris Johnston, who was elected as in MP in the 2015 General Election, was one of the leaders of the campaign to persuade people to vote to leave the EU in a referendum. The UK voted to leave the EU by 17,410,742 votes (51.9%) to 16,141,241 (48.1%). Prime Minister, David Cameron, who had campaigned to remain in the EU, resigned. The former Home Secretary, Theresa May, was elected to replace him as leader of the Conservative Party and became the UK's second woman Prime Minister. Labour MPs passed a vote of no-confidence in party leader, Jeremy Corbyn, but he survived a leadership challenge. MPs voted to renew Britain's nuclear weapons. Bank of England cut interest rates to .25%, the lowest level in their history. Great Britain finished 2nd in the medals table at the Olympic Games in Rio de Janeiro, behind USA.

2017 Martin McGuiness resigned a Northern Ireland's deputy First Minister in protest at First Minster Arlene Foster's refusal to resign over a costly scheme to encourage renewable energy, triggering an election in the Northern Ireland Assembly. No agreement was reached after the election and the Northern Ireland Executive was to remain suspended until 2020. European Union (Notification of Withdrawal) Act passed and May's Government invokes Article 50 of the EU Treaty, meaning that the UK would leave the European Union in 2 years' time. May then called a General Election to try to secure a bigger Conservative majority in the House of Commons. Instead the Conservatives lost their majority and May only remained in power with DUP support. In that election the Conservatives won 317 sets, Labour 232, SNP 35, Liberal Democrats 12 and DUP 10. Formal Brexit negotiations begun. Vince Cable became leader of Liberal Democrats. 71 people died in a fire at Grenfell Tower. Government said all diesel and petrol cars would be banned from 2040.

2018 Commonwealth leaders agreed that Prince Charles will succeed as Head of the Commonwealth on the death of the Queen. May's government suffered defeats in Parliament on its Brexit Bill. Prince Harry married Meghan Markle. May's Cabinet agree to negotiate a close relationship with the EU following Brexit, leading to the resignation of Brexit Secretary, David Davis, and Foreign Secretary, Boris Johnston, who both favoured a free trade agreement with the EU which did not tie the UK to EU rules. World's largest windfarm was built off Cumbria coast in northern England. May eventually secured EU agreement to her Brexit withdrawal proposals but could not get the agreement of Parliament. May won a no confidence vote on her leadership of the Conservative Party.

2019 The House of Commons rejects May's proposed withdrawal from the EU agreement by a large margin, but she survives a vote of confidence which would have triggered an election. The biggest difficulty to finding a Brexit agreement was the need to not have a customs boarder between the Republic of Ireland (which was remaining in the EU) and Northern Ireland (which was due to leave with the rest of the UK). 8 Labour MPs and 3 Conservative MPs resigned from their parties and formed The Independent Group. Labour decided to support a second referendum on leaving the EU. Extensions are agreed to the date when the UK will leave the EU to give more time to reach a deal. May announced intention to stand down before the next stage of the Brexit negotiations. Former UKIP leader, Nigel Farage, forms the Brexit Party. House of Commons was unable to agree on any Brexit withdrawal terms. Negotiations between Conservatives and Labour to try to agree withdrawal terms fail. In the European Parliamentary Election the new Brexit Party won 29 of the UK seats, the Liberal Democrats, who campaigned to keep the UK in the EU, won 16 seats, Labour won 10 seats, the Greens won 7 seats and the Conservatives won only 4 seats. May resigned and Boris Johnston was elected as leader of the Conservative Party and became Prime Minister. The UK had its hottest day on record. MPs opposing a Brexit without a deal with the EU took control of the House of Commons. Boris Johnston threw 21 Conservative MPs who voted against the government out of the Parliamentary party, and asked the Commons to approve his motion for a General Election. Under the Fixed Term Parliaments Act 2011 this motion required the support of two-thirds of MPs and the motion failed because Labour MPs would not vote in favour of it. The Supreme Court ruled that Johnston's request to the Queen to end the session of Parliament early was unlawful. Johnston's government reached agreement with the EU on a withdrawal agreement, but the DUP would not support it. Agreement is reached to extend the date for the UK's withdrawal from the EU to 31st January 2020. Jeremy Corbyn's Labour Party then supported a General Election, which was held on 12 December 2019. Johnson won a majority of 80 seats, while Labour had its worst result since 1935. In that election the Conservatives won 365 seats, Labour 202, SNP 48, Liberal Democrats 11, DUP 8 and others 16. The Brexit Party won no seats and Liberal Democrat Leader, Jo Swinson, lost her seat and resigned, with Ed Davey becoming the new leader. MPs voted in favour of the Brexit withdrawal agreement.

2020   The European Union formally agrees the Withdrawal Agreement and the EU Withdrawal Agreement Act is passed by Parliament. The UK leaves the European Union on 31st January, but remains in the single market and customs union for a further 11 months to allow time to negotiate a trade agreement with the EU. Significant flooding occurs in the early part of the year. A viral disease known as Covid-19, which was first detected in China in late 2019, spreads across the world. It often leads to severe respiratory problems, particularly in people over the age of 80 or who are suffering from other health issues. In response to growing numbers of deaths and hospital admissions a national lockdown is announced in March. There follows an extended period of travel restrictions and the closure of schools, and businesses which are not considered essential, in order to try to contain the spread of the virus and prevent the National Health Service being overwhelmed. Criminal penalties are introduced for persons who leave home without an essential reason, or who fail to wear masks and maintain a social distance from others in shops and other places. Sporting events are cancelled, and entertainment and hospitality venues closed. The Olympics due to take place in Japan is postponed until 2021. The Government provides financial aid to businesses and individuals worth hundreds of billions of pounds in an effort to support them through the pandemic. Sir Keir Starmer is elected leader of the Labour Party, replacing Jeremy Corbyn. The Welsh Assembly is renamed the Welsh Parliament, or Senedd Cymru. The economy shrinks and unemployment rises. Following the death of a black person in the United States, anti-racism protests occur in the United Kingdom, and a "Black Lives Matter" campaign enjoys large popular support. School exams are cancelled, with students awarded grades according to the predictions of their teachers. Work on producing new vaccines for Covid-19 is undertaken with great urgency around the world. The first vaccines are available by the end of the year and intensive efforts started to get everyone vaccinated, starting with the most vulnerable. The numbers of people with the virus dropped considerably by the Summer, allowing many restrictions to be lifted, and schools to reopen. However, new strains of the virus appeared, and numbers of new cases and deaths increased rapidly towards the year's end – resulting in the reintroduction of many lockdown measures and new school closures. The UK and the EU agree a free trade agreement at the end of the year, and the UK leaves the EU single market and customs union on 31st December.

ACKNOWLEDGMENTS

This book would not have been possible without the work of the many hundreds of historians down the ages who researched and recorded the facts which I have summarised here. I also thank the many artists who created the iconic historic images which I have been able to draw inspiration from, in my own meagre way, to illustrate these moments of British history. In many ways these are the real heroes of this work,

For the writing itself, I owe an eternal debt of gratitude to my wife, Terrie. She not only had to listen to and provide useful comments on the rhymes and commentaries that you see here, but also on all of the many earlier versions of the same!

Lilian Keller has dedicated a good chunk of her life in helping me bring this work to you, contributing many of the illustrations, as well as invaluable editorial and other assistance.

I thank Susan Harrison and Ale Calcioli for their work on the cover, and Grant Hudson for his additional drawings.

I sincerely hope that you have enjoyed reading it, and have forgiven me for some of the rhymes. I have tried to make the history understandable from reading the rhymes alone, and to do that I have had to take some unusual liberties. In the background commentaries I have tried not only to describe the 100 chosen moments, but also to sow these into the overall history of the last 1,000 years.

I hope I have inspired you to want to find out more.

Index of People

Catherine of Valois (Queen of England)	*1401-1437*	**1415, 1485**
William Caxton	*1422-1491*	**1477**
Robert Cecil (Earl of Salisbury)	*1563-1612*	**1603**
Neville Chamberlain	*1869-1940*	**1939, 1940**
Prince Charles of Wales (Duke of Cornwall)	*1948-*	**1952, 1997, 2005, 2015**
King Charles I	*1600-1649*	**1640, 1660, 1840**
King Charles II	*1630-1685*	**1660, 1665, 1666, 1687, 1688, 1711**
Charles IV (King of France)	*1294-1328*	**1337**
Charles VI (King of France)	*1368-1422*	**1415**
Charles VII (King of France)	*1403-1461*	**1415**
Geoffrey Chaucer	*1343-1400*	**1387, 1477**
Winston Churchill	*1874-1965*	**1940, 1945, 1952**
Lord Randolph Churchill	*1911-1968*	**1940**
Nick Clegg	*1967-*	**2007, 2010, 2015**
Christopher Columbus	*1451-1506*	**1620**
John Constable	*1776-1837*	**1838**
Captain James Cook	*1728-1779*	**1770**
William Cooke	*1806-1879*	**1875**
Jeremy Corbyn	*1949-*	**2015, 2016**
Francis Crick	*1916-2004*	**1953**
Oliver Cromwell	*1599-1658*	**1640, 1660**
Richard Cromwell	*1626-1712*	**1660**
Thomas Cromwell	*1485-1540*	**1509, 1533**
Duke of Cumberland (Prince William)	*1721-1765*	**1746**
Alistair Darling	*1953-*	**2008**
Lord Darnley (Henry Stuart)	*1545-1567*	**1587**
Charles Darwin	*1809-1882*	**1859, 1953**
Erasmus Darwin	*1731-1802*	**1859**
Ed Davey	*1965-*	**2019**
Humphry Davey	*1778-1829*	**1831**
David I (King of Scotland)	*1084-1153*	**1603**
King David II of Scotland	*1324-1371*	**1348**
David Davis	*1948-*	**2018**
Emily Davison	*1872-1913*	**1913**
Charles De Gaulle (French President)	*1890-1970*	**1973**
Simon de Montford	*1208-1265*	**1265, 1283**
Despenser Family		**1327**
Princess Diana of Wales (Diana Spencer)	*1961-1997*	**1997**
Charles Dickens	*1812-1870*	**1839**
Benjamin Disraeli (Earl of Beaconsfield)	*1804-1881*	**1876**
Sir Alec Douglas-Home	*1903-1995*	**1962**
Sir Frances Drake	*c1540-1596*	**1588**
Anthony Eden	*1897-1977*	**1962**
Edmund Tudor (Earl of Richmond)	*1430-1456*	**1485**
King Edmund II (Edmund Ironside of Wessex)	*993-1016*	**1028**
Edmund of Langley (Duke of York)	*1341-1402*	**1415, 1455**
Edward (Duke of Kent)	*1767-1820*	**1837**
King Edward the Confessor	*1003-1066*	**1055, 1066, 1085**
Prince Edward (Earl of Wessex)	*1964-*	**1952**
King Edward I (Edward Longshanks)	*1239-1307*	**1265, 1283, 1314**

King Edward II	*1284-1327*	**1314, 1327**
King Edward III	*1312-1377*	**1096, 1314, 1327, 1337, 1348**
King Edward IV	*1442-1483*	**1455, 1477, 1483. 1509**
King Edward V	*1470-c1483*	**1055, 1483, 1485**
King Edward VI	*1537-1553*	**1509, 1553, 1587**
King Edward VII	*1841-1910*	**1899, 1901**
King Edward VIII (Duke of Windsor)	*1894-1972*	**1055, 1936, 1952**
Edward Elgar	*1857-1934*	**1899**
Queen Elizabeth I	*1533-1603*	**1509, 1553, 1587, 1588, 1591, 1603, 1611, 1876**
Queen Elizabeth II	*1926-*	**1952, 2012, 2018**
Elizabeth of York (Queen of England)	*1466-1503*	**1485, 1509**
Elizabeth Woodville (Queen of England)	*1437-1492*	**1483**
Princess Elizabeth (Elizabeth Stuart)	*1596-1662*	**1605**
Ernest Augustus (King of Hanover)	*1771-1851*	**1837**
Pope Eugene III	*1088-1153*	**1154**
Eustace (Eustace IV, Count of Boulogne)	*1130-1153*	**1135**
Michael Faraday	*1791-1867*	**1831, 1865, 1875, 1989**
Nigel Farage	*1964-*	**2014, 2019**
Tim Farron	*1970-*	**2015**
Guy Fawkes	*1570-1606*	**1605**
Dodi Fayed	*1955-1997*	**1997**
Walter FitzAlan	*c1106-1177*	**1603**
Alexander Fleming	*1881-1955*	**1928**
King Sweyn Forkbeard	*960-1014*	**1028**
Arlene Foster	*1970-*	**2016, 2017**
Francis II (King of France)	*1544-1560*	**1587**
General Franco	*1892-1975*	**1939**
Piers Gavestone	*1284-1312*	**1327**
Geoffrey of Anjou	*1113-1151*	**1135**
Geoffrey (Duke of Aquitaine)	*1158-1186*	**1189**
David Lloyd George	*1863-1945*	**1911, 1913, 1924, 1940**
Prince George of Cambridge	*2013-*	**2013**
King George I	*1660-1727*	**1714, 1721, 1746**
King George II	*1683-1760*	**1746**
King George III	*1738-1820*	**1776, 1796, 1837, 1838**
King George IV (Prince Regent)	*1762-1830*	**1796, 1832**
King George V	*1865-1936*	**1911, 1913, 1924, 1936, 1952**
King George VI	*1895-1952*	**1936, 1940, 1952**
William Gladstone	*1809-1898*	**1870, 1876**
Godwin (Earl of Wessex)	*1001-1053*	**1066**
Lord Grenville (William Grenville)	*1759-1834*	**1807**
Earl Grey (Charles Grey)	*1764-1845*	**1832, 1837**
Lady Jane Grey	*1537-1554*	**1553**
Johannes Gutenberg	*c1400-1468*	**1477**
Lord Halifax (Edward Wood)	*1881-1959*	**1940**
Harald Hardrada (King of Norway)	*1015-1066*	**1066**
King Hardicanute (Canute III)	*c1018-1042*	**1028, 1055**
Keir Hardie	*1856-1915*	**1924**
King Harold I (Harold Harefoot)	*c1016-1040*	**1028**
King Harold II (Harold Godwinson)	*c1022-1066*	**1055, 1066**

Prince Harry (Duke of Sussex)	1984-	1997, 2018
Anne Hathaway	1556-1623	1591
Edward Heath	1916-2005	1973, 1979
Heinrich V (Holy Roman Emperor)	c1081-1125	1135
Heinrich VI (Holy Roman Emperor)	1165-1197	1189
Henry the Young King	1155-1183	1189
Henry Fitzroy (Duke of Richmond)	1519-1536	1509
Henry of Huntingdon	c1088-c1157	1028
King Henry I	c1068-1135	1100
King Henry II (Henry FitzEmpress)	1133-1189	1096, 1135, 1154, 1170, 1189, 1800
King Henry III	1207-1272	1055, 1215, 1233, 1265, 1283
King Henry IV (Henry Bolingbroke)	1367-1413	1387, 1415, 1455, 1591
King Henry V	1386-1422	1415, 1455, 1477, 1485, 1591
King Henry VI	1421-1471	1415, 1455, 1485
King Henry VII	1457-1509	1485, 1509, 1603
King Henry VIII	1491-1547	1509, 1533, 1553, 1587, 1611, 1800, 1840
Adolf Hitler	1889-1945	1939, 1940, 1945
Gustav Holst	1874-1934	1899
Catherine Howard (Queen of England)	c1523-1542	1509
Geoffrey Howe	1926-2015	1990
William Huskisson	1770-1830	1804
Isabella of France (Queen of England)	1295-1358	1327, 1337
King James I (James VI of Scotland)	1566-1625	1587, 1591, 1603, 1605, 1611, 1620, 1640, 1770
King James II (James VII of Scotland)	1633-1701	1688, 1694, 1707, 1714, 1746
James IV of Scotland	1473-1513	1587, 1603
James V of Scotland	1512-1542	1587
Jane Seymour (Queen of England)	c1508-1537	1509
Edward Jenner	1749-1823	1796
Joan of Arc	c1412-1431	1337
King John	1166-1216	1189, 1215, 1265,1591, 1800
John of Gaunt (Duke of Lancaster)	1340-1399	1387, 1415, 1455, 1485
Boris Johnston	1964-	2008, 2012, 2016, 2018, 2019
Sadiq Khan	1970-	2016
Lord Kitchener	1850-1916	1902
Earl of Lancaster (Thomas)	1278-1322	1327
John Lennon	1940-1980	1962
Duke Leopold V of Austria	1157-1194	1189
Llywelyn ap Gruffydd (Prince of Wales)	1223-1282	1283
Louis XVI (King of France)	1754-1793	1805
Louis XVIII (King of France)	1755-1824	1815
Martin Luther	1483-1546	1533
Ramsey MacDonald	1866-1937	1924, 1936
Harold Macmillan	1894-1986	1962
John Major	1943-	1990
Margaret of York (Duchess of Burgundy)	1446-1503	1477
Guglielmo Marconi	1874-1937	1925
Princess Margaret (Countess of Snowdon)	1930-2002	1952
Meghan Markle (Duchess of Sussex)	1981-	2018

Queen Mary I	*1516-1558*	**1509, 1553, 1588**
Queen Mary II	*1662-1694*	**1688, 1689, 1694, 1707**
Mary Queen of Scots (Queen of France)	*1542-1587*	**1587, 1588, 1603**
Empress Matilda	*1102-1167*	**1135**
James Clerk Maxwell	*1831-1879*	**1865, 1925**
Theresa May	*1965-*	**2016, 2017**
Paul McCartney	*1942-*	**1962**
Martin McGuinness	*1950-2017*	**2007, 2017**
Catherine Middleton (Duchess of Cambridge)	*1982-*	**2011, 2013**
Ed Milliband	*1969-*	**2010, 2015**
George Monck (Duke of Albemarle)	*1608-1670*	**1660**
Claude Monet	*1840-1926*	**1838**
Sir Thomas More	*1478-1535*	**1509, 1533**
Samuel Morse	*1791-1872*	**1875**
Roger Mortimer (Earl of March)	*1287-1330*	**1327, 1337**
Benito Mussolini	*1883-1945*	**1939**
Lord Nelson	*1758-1805*	**1805, 1838, 1912**
Thomas Newcomen	*1664-1729*	**1769**
Sir Isaac Newton	*1643-1727*	**1687, 1859**
Florence Nightingale	*1820-1910*	**1855**
Earl of Oxford (John de Vere)	*1442-1513*	**1485**
Lord Palmerston (Henry Temple)	*1784-1865*	**1870**
Emmeline Pankhurst	*1858-1928*	**1913**
Catherine Parr (Queen of England)	*1512-1548*	**1509**
Ian Paisley	*1926-2014*	**2007**
Sir Robert Peel	*1788-1850*	**1837**
Samuel Pepys	*1633-1703*	**1666**
Spencer Perceval	*1762-1812*	**1990**
Prince Philip (Duke of Edinburgh)	*1921-2021*	**1952**
Philip Augustus II (King of France)	*1165-1223*	**1215**
Philip II of Spain (King consort of England)	*1527-1598*	**1533, 1588**
Philip III of Spain	*1578-1621*	**1605**
Philip VI of France (Philip of Valios)	*1293-1350*	**1337**
William Pitt the Younger	*1759-1806*	**1800, 1807**
Thomas Pride	*c1610-1658*	**1640**
Sir Walter Raleigh	*1552-1618*	**1620**
King Richard I	*1157-1199*	**1189**
Richard of Shrewsbury (Duke of York)	*1473-c1483*	**1483**
King Richard II	*1367-1400*	**1381, 1387, 1415,1455**
King Richard III (Duke of Gloucester)	*1452-1485*	**1483, 1485, 1591**
Robert II (King of Scotland)	*1316-1390*	**1603**
Robert of Normandy	*1051-1106*	**1100**
Robert the Bruce (King of Scotlland)	*1274-1329*	**1314, 1327**
General Rommel	*1891-1944*	**1945**
John Ruskin	*1819-1900*	**1838**
Saddam Hussein	*1937-2006*	**2003**
Saladin (Sultan of Egypt & Syria)	*1138-1193*	**1189**
Lord Salisbury (Robert Gascoyne-Cecil)	*1830-1903*	**1901, 1912**
Alex Salmond	*1954-*	**2007, 2011, 2012, 2014**
John Shakespeare	*1531-1601*	**1591**
William Shakespeare	*1564-1616*	**1591**

Name	Dates	Years
Wallis Simpson (Duchess of Windsor)	1896-1986	1936
Sophia of Hanover	1630-1714	1714
St Peter (Simon Peter, Peter the Apostle)	c1-c64	1154
Josef Stalin	1878-1953	1939, 1945
Lord Stanley (Thomas Stanley)	1435-1504	1485
Sir Keir Starmer	1962-	2020
King Stephen (Stephen Blois)	1092-1154	1135
Robert Stephenson	1803-1859	1804
Charles Stuart (Bonnie Prince Charles)	1720-1788	1746
James Stuart (The Old Pretender)	1688-1766	1688, 1746
Nicola Sturgeon	1970-	2014
Jo Swinson	1980-	2019
Margaret Thatcher	1925-2013	1979, 1982, 1990
Theobald of Bec	1090-1161	1170
Tostig Godwinson	c1023-1066	1066
Richard Trevithick	1771-1833	1804
Jasper Tudor (Duke of Bedford)	1431-1495	1485
Owen Tudor	1400-1461	1485
Margaret Tudor (Queen consort of Scotland)	1489-1541	1587
Alan Turing	1912-1954	1989
JMW Turner	1775-1851	1838
Wat Tyler	1341-1381	1381
Queen Victoria	1819-1901	1837, 1840, 1851, 1876, 1901, 1952
William Wallace	1270-1305	1314
Robert Walpole	1676-1745	1721
Earl of Warwick (Richard Neville)	1428-1471	1455
George Washington	1732-1799	1776
James Watson	1928-	1953
Thomas Watson	1854-1934	1875
James Watt	1736-1819	1769, 1804
Duke of Wellington (Arthur Wellesley)	1769-1852	1815
Charles Wheatstone	1802-1875	1875
William Wilberforce	1759-1833	1807
Kaiser Wilhelm I (German Emperor)	1797-1888	1912
Kaiser Wilhelm II (German Emperor)	1859-1941	1918
Prince William (Duke of Cambridge)	1982-	1997, 2011, 2013
King William I (William the Conqueror)	1028-1087	1066, 1085, 1096, 1100
William II (William Rufus)	1060-1100	1096, 1100
King William III (William of Orange)	1650-1702	1688, 1689, 1694, 1707
King William IV	1765-1837	1832, 1837
Henry Willink	1894-1973	1948
Harold Wilson	1916-1995	1962, 1973, 1979
Cardinal Wolsey (Thomas Wolsey)	1473-1530	1509, 1533
Sir Christopher Wren	1632-1723	1711
Thomas Wyatt	1521-1554	1553

GLOSSARY

Abbot	Head of a building occupied by a group of monks, known as an abbey
Abdicate	Formally give up a crown.
Accord	Agreement
Act	A written law made by Parliament and consented to by the monarch
Anglo-Saxons	Tribes originating from Angeln and Saxony, in what is now Germany, who invaded England in the 5th Century AD and took over.
Annexing	Taking someone else's land and adding it to one's own
Apocrypha	Some Christian writings included in early bibles, but considered to have doubtful validity and usually now omitted
Appeasement	Trying to keep the peace by agreeing to demands
Archbishop	A chief bishop. The Church of England has two Archbishops, the Archbishop of Canterbury and the Archbishop of York.
Archdeacon	A senior Christian priest
Atom	The smallest particle of an element
Avert	Prevent something happening
Balkans	An area of south east Europe, consisting of Bosnia, Bulgaria and most of Greece and Serbia, and surrounding areas.
Baroness	A female member of the House of Lords
Baron	A male lord
Binary	A system of numbers using only 1s and 0s, also known as base 2.
Bishop	A senior Christian clergyman, responsible for a region.
Borough	A town or settlement that was granted some self-government. Originally the term referred to a walled town.
Bourbon	A European royal House originating in France, whose different branches held thrones across Europe for centuries, including in France, Spain and Italy
Bubonic	Causing a swelling under the armpits or groin
Burgess	A free citizen of a town or borough
Cabinet	Group of senior ministers who control government policy.
Carbon-based	The element carbon is found in significant quantity in all life forms. Most fuels come from life forms, such as wood, or the residue from ancient life forms, such as coal or oil. Such fuels are said to be carbon-based, and when they burn give off carbon dioxide.
Cardinal	A leading priest of the Catholic Church ranking next below the Pope and appointed by him.
Cavalier	A supporter of King Charles I during the Civil War. The word originally meant "horseman" but came to mean someone who was reckless. It was first applied to Charles I supporters by his opponents as a term of abuse.

Centrist	A person with moderate political views.
Charter	A written grant giving rights and privileges
Clergyman	A priest or other minister of a Church
Coalition	A joining together of different political parties to form a government
Coarser	More rude or vulgar
Colonise	Create a settlement in a place and take control over any existing inhabitants
Communism	A political system based on the idea that all property is owned by the community and each person contributes and receives according to their ability and needs. Communist rulers and governments exercise extensive control over the lives of their citizens.
Community charge	A tax in the United Kingdom set at the same amount for every adult by local authorities to pay for local government, which existed from 1989 to 1993. Also known as the Poll Tax.
Conciliatory	Intended or likely to gain agreement or goodwill from someone who is hostile.
Confessor	Someone who seeks forgiveness from God for wrongful acts and sins they have committed, indicating a strong religious faith.
Conjecture	A conclusion based on incomplete information
Conscientious	Wanting to do the right thing
Conservative	Someone who opposes radical change and supports traditional values. Also refers to the members of the Conservative Party.
Consort	The husband of a ruling Queen. Can also refer to the wife of a King, although they are usually called Queen.
Constituency	A group of people who can elect a representative for an area, or the area itself.
Constitutional	According to an established set of principles or laws
County	A large area with its own local administration, known as county councils. Historically England was divided into 39 counties, but following reorganisations there are currently 48.
Courtiers	A person who often attends a royal court to give advice or companionship to a monarch.
Crimean	Relating to the Crimea, which is a peninsular on the North side of the Black Sea
Crusade	One of a series of military expeditions by Christian Europeans to try to conquer and install Christian control of Jerusalem and the area of the middle east where Jesus Christ was said to have lived, known as the Holy Land.
Dauphin	Eldest son of King of France, and heir to the throne
Debtor's Prison	Prisons formerly for people who owed money. Such people were usually kept in prison until the debt was paid.
Decimalisation	A change to a currency based on 10s and 100s. After Britain decimalised a pound consisted of 100 new pennies, whereas before a pound consisted of 20 shillings and a shilling consisted of 12 old pennies.
Delegation	A group of people appointed to do something as representatives of some cause, person or larger group

Deposed	Removed from a position of power by force
Devolved	Having had power in certain areas transferred to it by a higher level of government
Dispensation	Having been freed from an obligation or rule that is imposed on others
DNA	Short for Deoxyribose Nucleic Acid. It is called nucleic acid because it is acidic and was first found in the nucleus of living cells. Deoxyribose refers to one of its important components. It consists of two chains of a sugar (called deoxyribose) and phosphate which coil around each other in a double helix, and are joined together by millions of paired molecules of cytosine(C), guanine (G), adenine (A) and thymine (T) – which are known as base pairs. These four joining molecules consist of hydrogen, nitrogen and oxygen atoms in different combinations. C only pairs with G, and A only pairs with T. The sequence of the base pairs in DNA determines the genetic code of all living things.
Dominion Status	Given the power of complete self-government within the British Empire. The word dominion means sovereignty or control.
Dreadnought	A type of battleship in the early 1900s which was considerably bigger and more powerful than earlier battelships.
Duke	A title given to a Lord holding the highest rank of nobility.
Earl	A title given to a Lord holding a rank of nobility below Duke and Marquess, but above Viscounts and Baron. In England it was the highest rank until 1337.
Effigy	A roughly made model of someone, particularly someone who is hated, for the purposes of making a protest.
Electorate	All the people in an area or country who are allowed to vote in an election.
Emancipation	Being freed from legal or other restrictions
Eminent	Famous or highly respected in a given field
Empress	A female ruler of an empire. An empire consists of a number of states or countries
Entente Cordial	A friendly alliance between Britain and France which began in the early 1900s
Exchequer	The national treasury. Usually refers to the money held by and available to a government.
Exploits	Bold or heroic actions.
Feudal	The word feudal derives from a Latin word for a fee or payment for services. In the feudal system people were provided with land in return for loyalty and service.
First Lord of the Admiralty	The member of the government responsible for the Royal Navy
Free Trade	International buying and selling of goods without special taxes or restrictions
Funnel	A chimney, usually made out of metal, for a steam engine or ship
Gamma Rays	Electromagnetic waves with a very short wavelength given off by decaying atoms, known as radiation
Gentry	Persons of high social position, but below the nobility.

Geologist	Person who studies the physical substance of the earth and how it got that way
Great Depression	Severe economic conditions suffered by countries around the world from late 1929 through the 1930s.
Guerrilla	Member of a military group fighting against an established force, often using unconventional means.
Guildhall	A hall originally used for meetings of associations of merchants or craftsmen (known as guilds)
Harried	Harassed or annoyed by persistent acts of another
Heretic	A person holding a religious belief contrary to the established belief.
High Middle Ages	The Middle Ages (or medieval period) refers to a period of European history from the fall of the Roman Empire to the Renaissance (which means rebirth). It is broken into 3 periods – Early Middle Ages (or the Dark Ages) from about 500-1000 AD, High Middle Ages from about 1000-1250 AD and Late Middle Ages from about 1250-1500 AD
Holding	An area of land usually held by a lease
Homage	Deep respect shown publicly. To pay homage to another meant to formally acknowledge that they are one's lord, to whom one owes loyalty and service.
Home Rule	The government of a country or region, which is part of a larger power, by its own people.
Home Secretary	Senior Government Minister in charge of the Home Office – which is the government department responsible for law and order and the control of borders
House of Commons	One of the two houses of Parliament, whose members are elected by the people.
House of Lords	One of the two houses of Parliament, whose members are not elected, consisting of Lords and Bishops.
HRH	His Royal Highness or Her Royal Highness. Refers to senior members of the royal family, but not the monarch -who is referred to as His or Her Majesty.
Humble	Being of low importance or rank, or acting as though you are.
Imperialist	Someone who believes in countries expanding their power by colonising other countries and creating an empire
Landslide victory	Winning by a large majority in an election
Left wing	In politics this refers to people and political parties who support social equality. The term originated from the French National Assembly in 1789, in which nobles sat on the right and "common" people on the left.
Liberal	Someone who supports individual liberty and freedoms. Also a member of the Liberal Party which traditionally supported reform, democracy and free trade.
Light Brigade	A British Army force mounted on horseback with no armour, allowing for rapid attacks.
Lime	A white substance made of calcium and oxygen which burns easily and has many uses in building and manufacturing.

Long parliament	A Parliament originally called by King Charles I in 1640 which lasted until 1660.
Lord	A title given to barons and more senior members of the nobility. In early times they were given authority over particular regions and peoples by the monarch. Their title is usually passed down to their eldest surviving son on their death. "The Lord" refers to Jesus Christ, who is considered to be the son of God by Christians and to have authority over everyone, including Kings and Queens.
Lord Chancellor	A senior government minister responsible for the Courts and the legal system. Formerly known as the Lord High Chancellor, he was the most powerful officer of the Crown.
Maastricht Treaty	The Maastricht Treaty was agreed by the member states of the European Community in 1991, and was responsible for the creation of the European Union in 1993.
Magna Carta	Magna Carta refers to the Great Charter signed by King John in 1215 guaranteeing certain fundamental rights to his subjects
Monarch	The sovereign head of a country, usually a King or Queen.
Monastery	A place of residence of a community of monks living by religious rules.
Money Bills	A proposed Parliamentary Act which concerns taxation or government spending
Monk	A member of a religious community of men living according to religious rules.
Mortar	A mixture of lime, clay, sand and water which is used to bind bricks or stones together in building.
Mounted	Undertook a significant course of action
Naturalist	Student of natural history, involving the observation of animals and plants
Neutron	One of the 3 components of an atom, the others being electrons and protons.
New Model Army	The Army formed by the Parliamentary side in 1645, during the English Civil War.
New Testament	The part of the Bible consisting of a collection of books containing the story of Jesus Christ (known as the Gospels) and Christian teachings
Nobility (Nobles, Noblemen)	Refers to persons considered to be high born and having a title of Baron or above, and their immediate family
Norman	A member of a group of people, being a mix of Vikings from Scandinavia, and Frankish who settled in Northwest France, in what became Normandy, from the early 900s, and their descendants.
Noxious	Poisonous or causing considerable discomfort
Office of State	One of the 4 most senior positions in the British government, which are now Prime Minister, Chancellor of the Exchequer, Foreign Secretary and Home Secretary. Can also refer to other senior positions, such as Lord High Chancellor, particularly in earlier times.
Old Testament	The earlier part of the Christian Bible consisting of a collection books which describe the Creation of the universe and the story of the Hebrews before the birth of Jesus Christ. This corresponds approximately to the Jewish (Hebrew) Bible.

Orator	A public speaker
Ottoman	An empire founded originally in about 1299 by the Turkish leader Osman I. It is named after him, as his name in Arabic was "Othman"
Ousted	Expelled from a position
Overlord	A person who is the lord of other lords, such as a king
Paddle-wheel	A wheel made of many boards, which propels a ship through water by turning.
Panama	A country in Central America
Papacy	The position or power of the Pope, who is the leader of the Catholic Church.
Papal	Relating to the Pope
Parson	A priest with responsibility for a small local area.
Patent	A right, granted by the government, to make exclusive use of an invention for a period of time.
Patron	A person who gives financial or other support to another
Patronage	The support of a patron
Penal	Concerned with punishment of criminals
Pestilence	A deadly spreading disease
Pilgrim	A person who travels somewhere for religious reasons
Political	Concerned with politics. Politics refers to activities concerned with the government of a country or group.
Pomp	A splendid display
Prince Regent	A regent is someone appointed to rule for a period of time because a monarch is unable to do so. The son of a monarch who performs this role is called a Prince Regent.
Prowess	Particular skill or expertise
Puritan	A member of an English Protestant movement in the 16th and 17th Centuries who favoured further reform away from the Catholic Church to simpler and "purer" forms of religious worship
Ravage	Severely damage
Rearm	Build up stores of weapons and military equipment again
Referendum	A vote by an electorate on a question in order to reach a decision.
Reform	Make changes intended to improve something
Right wing	In politics this refers to people and political parties who support social inequality. The term originated from the French National Assembly in 1789, in which nobles sat on the right and "common" people on the left.
Interregnum	A period where a throne is vacant and there is no monarch.
Republic	A form of government in which the head of state is elected or nominated rather than a monarch.
Repugnant	Objectionable or unacceptable

Roundheads	The name given to Parliamentary supporters during the English Civil War. The term was a reference to the short-cropped hairstyle of Puritans, who made up an important part of the Parliamentary party.
Royal Mint	The place where coins were officially manufactured
Royalist Armies	Armies supporting the cause of the monarch
Rudimentary	Basic or fundamental
Rump	A small part left of something that was once larger
Scandinavia	An area of northern Europe consisting of Norway, Sweden and Denmark.
Scorched Earth Policy	A military strategy involving the deliberate destruction of crops and other resources that might assist an invading army.
Succession	The process of passing a title or crown to another, usually by inheritance on death.
Serfdom	A system where labourers, known as serfs, were required to work on their lord's estate
Socialism	A political system where the means of production and distribution are owned by the community as a whole.
Spurned	Rejected with disdain
Statute	An Act or written law passed by Parliament.
Subjects	A citizen of a state other than the ruler
Subsumed	Absorbed into something else
Suez	A shipping canal, running through Egypt, which connects the Mediterranean Sea to the Red Sea and the Indian Ocean.
Test Acts	A series of laws which restricted public offices and other positions to members of the Church of England, known as a religious test.
Tories	Originally the name given to politicians who supported traditional values and social order. A name now given to members of the Conservative Party.
Transistors	A device used to increase or switch electrical signals.
Treaty	A formal written agreement between two or more countries
Tribe	A group of people linked by common ties of community, often having a single leader.
Tudor	The English Royal House and the period in which they held the English crown from 1485 to 1603.
Union	A Trade Union is a workers' organisation which seeks to better the lives of its members by securing better conditions and pay. The term union means the joining together of things
Uranium	A dense metallic element used as a fuel in nuclear reactors
Usurper	A person who takes something over illegally
Veto	To prevent something
Vikings	Scandinavians who raided and settled in north west Europe from the 8th Century

Virulent	Extremely severe or harmful
Welfare State	A system in which the state protects the well-being of its citizens in need.
Whigs	A political grouping from the late 17th Century of persons favouring reform, which evolved into the Liberal Party.

Printed in Great Britain
by Amazon

63547257R00149